MY LESBIAN MOM IN THE 90S
A SON'S JOURNEY TO ACCEPTANCE

D. E. CUPERTINO

First Edition

DEDICATION

I would like to dedicate my work to my grandparents;
Yesterday, I realized why my mom and I love you so much. I think it's
because you have always loved us, without judgement, without
reservation, just pure authentic love.

TABLE OF CONTENTS

PREFACE

Initially I was reluctant to publish this story. I knew that after publishing this story the world would know my entire life. I have always been a private person, scared to show the real me. Still here I am, the story of my mom and I comes with great pain and suffering. Mom and I collaborated on this book together. In me releasing this, she will reveal personal aspects about her life, as will I. She is okay with that. Before I began writing the book I gave her a full disclosure, and with her consent and knowledge I wrote this book. She has accompanied me on this road, it has been a long time coming and every step of the way has been worth it. My goal is not to hurt my mom at all, that was the furthest thing from what my intention was while writing this book. It was more than difficult at times to reminisce, but the process was very healing for us. Many people ask about what homosexual couples think of having children in today's society, but no one ever asks what the children think of it. My mom and I agree that this is a discussion that needs to be had. We also both agreed some time ago that we wanted to get everything out in the open, in the hopes of helping other people who have lived similar pasts.

However, not all pasts are this difficult. All things considered, every past and every person has something to give. Having said this, our story today comes with many tears and pain, and it can still be shared with whoever can gain from it. This is our gift to you, the reader, with the hope that our message touches your soul and heart in an authentic way. Our hope is that our story creates dialogue and conversation about our personal humanity. When I told my grandfather about my undertaking in writing this book he said, "Daniel, I'm not sure that you should publish this book. Just make sure your mom doesn't get hurt, she loves you." He also told me to consider, "What if it isn't successful?" I have seriously considered what my grandpa has said. Therefore, I have thoroughly invested myself in completing this book, despite the uncertainty of the outcome. In short, I am willingly taking a big step into the unknown…Much of my life I spent unable to express myself. It was the same case with my mom. I was unable to accept my mom, but that was such an easy choice since we didn't have real and open conversations about her sexuality. This book is just about being real and honest. Since light scatters darkness, mom and I are hoping to scatter darkness in our lives, and we hope this for many others also. With the light, it becomes necessary to face some hard truths. Hopefully you will understand where I'm coming from, and hopefully you will understand where my mom is coming from. There may be some points within the book that you may not agree with, and there may be some subjects as well, that in my opinion aren't discussed enough, which are difficult to face so I ask that you keep an open mind and complete the story. Take this message forever with you, strength, love and commitment, in your heart.

I believe in order to understand others we must first take away our pride and then we humble ourselves, to listen to the heart, to listen to the soul, and then we will begin to love. This is a journey and journeys are a shared thing, they are never completed in solitude. So here is my journey, and here is my mom's journey.

INTRODUCTION

As a millennial growing up in the 90s it simply meant, being a kid. The simple pleasures of life were many. I enjoyed playing outside often, I spent a significant amount of time watching Nickelodeon, being entertained and educated by Mrs. Frizzle's Magic School Bus at school. For the generation immediately before us millennials, it was a prosperous time as the U.S. economy was bolstering and adults were awaiting the dawn of a new millennium. Meanwhile, I wasn't simply occupied with these simple pleasures only because they were readily available. I was just a kid enjoying them, but they were a great distraction because I missed my mother much of the time. Due to certain circumstances, my father was not in my life. I don't think her absence directly correlates with her being lesbian but they were closely linked. I didn't sing "Scooby Dooby Doo where are you?" I thought rather, "Mom where are you?" I found the answer the more I searched. It was and is still to this day a good, but arduous journey.

My mom is a lesbian and as her son I have only told three people outside of my family. One might ask why? I think I've always felt some kind of shame or embarrassment especially as a kid. I didn't understand her. I didn't understand where she was coming from. We never spoke of it. One constant thought in my mind was that we were living in a small town, where most of the people come from a religious background and traditional Christian values. So one could imagine that this would be difficult or nearly impossible to express openly. The silence at times was unbearable.

How did I deal with this as a kid? I just didn't. It was easier that way. So as one can imagine having a lesbian mom, no father, no siblings, and a Mormon best friend was hard to balance as a kid, as much as I could be aware of all of these people and factors at that time. I just wanted to fit in. Don't we all? How could I fit in though? I was so different, I suppose one could say I judged her because at the time I felt like she made it impossible for me to be normal. She placed me in a position where I was different from others, so that was the blame that I shifted onto her. My mom loved me unconditionally, but she was still maturing as a woman and she didn't know how to express her love at times. She didn't know how to be a parent. As a result she was unaware of the state that I was in. In addition to her lack of parental maturity, there were several other circumstances at play. Circumstances such as, her personal maturation process, her being a single mother, and her legitimately attempting to explore romance, though this was in an avenue that I definitely didn't understand. I always wanted what I thought a traditional family should be like. I just never understood why she wanted that lifestyle for us. To me it never felt right, so I always tried to escape my own reality. I think as a kid one would want to be a little different in a good way, to stick out, you know? However, I think it is very easy for children to become misdirected in their efforts to be noticed, as many parents would agree. I gradually grew from this desire to be accepted to being who I am, and my mother could also dare to hope that I could one day forgive her. Through time and dialogue my mother and I are on a more solid footing.

This understanding of one another came with a few shocks though. I thought that I was the only one to suffer neglect or loneliness as a kid. Sometimes it takes understanding of another person to be understood. My mother has endured many trials as well that have set the dynamic of pain and isolation for the both of us. When I began to discover my mother's past and I began to know her more, it shook me. The love and understanding for one another has grown as a direct result of each other's efforts to come to better terms with one another. This is only a product of one another's willingness to be open and to try to understand each other more thoroughly. We are adults still growing independently, but still we are accompanying each other on this road called life. Hopefully we may meet our loved ones as they are, and just be there for one another. So journey with my mother and I, and hopefully this can help bridge some gaps between you and your loved ones, if need be.

CHAPTER 1
SMALL TOWN GIRL

Small towns are a peculiar thing if you haven't had the fortune to grow up in one or live in one, it is a good atmosphere to place yourself in. To those of us that have grown up in small towns, they can bring a unique perspective, focused on simplicity especially the simple pleasures of life. My grandparents tell me that one of the more singular aspects that are found in small town America is the cohesiveness that small towns possess. If a person's car breaks down, people would readily give a helping hand. There are also instances where people chip in if a person in the community is diagnosed with a terminal illness with medical costs or with funeral expenses. Proximity to neighbors is a staple and this is still true today. Small towns have evolved in the United States but these hallmarks are still common place in Holbrook, Arizona or in Russellville, Alabama. Some of these towns across America have had their challenges as far as the proliferation of drugs, and economic struggle of the poor and middle class. Smaller towns generally have a more mellow feel to them, and this helps people who live in them to stop and consider the deeper and more meaningful things in life. My grandparents both grew up in small towns, my mother grew up in a small town and still lives in one, and I have bounced around but small town America has had just a meaningful impact on my life as it has on my mom and grandparents' own lives. We all take experiences in differently than the next person, and this is the story of how I have taken in my own experiences up until now. This is my journey to understanding myself and my mother, and accepting us both for who we are.

My grandfather was born in New Mexico in a small farming town just outside of Albuquerque. His story is particularly interesting because grandpa was always a simple and hardworking man. He grew up in simple time having been born in 1929. He had a rough upbringing, he got his extraordinary work ethic from his parents but neither of them showed him much love. Yes it was a simpler time and one indication of this is that he dropped out of school at fourteen to help his family. At around age sixteen he moved to McNary, Arizona to work at a saw mill plant. "I had never seen so much money in my life, after paying my expenses I would send the rest back home." he told me. He lead a simple life of work, prayer, and the occasional movie or stroll outside with friends in the snow. Life centered around obtaining the basic necessities for survival and enjoying the small things in life. Suddenly his rhythm of life was altered. He didn't have a clue that this is where he would meet his wife.

My grandmother was born in Texas, but a few short days later she and her family moved to McNary, Arizona where she grew up. In contrast to my grandfather, she came from a very warm loving home and this molded and shaped her for the rest of her life. This helped her become an amazing housewife. One day my grandfather had just left work, and he had heard that there was a high school graduation ceremony happening that evening. He decided to go to the graduation ceremony the town was holding, and this decision would prove to be fortuitous. He was struck by how eloquently the salutatorian had spoken at the ceremony, but more so by her simple elegance. He really liked her. Grandpa had noticed her a couple more times after that and then he decided that he would follow her on her way to work. There was an innocence there that is all too rare in our days, he didn't have a single malicious thought, he was only a young guy that was smitten by a beautiful young woman. Once they met he decided to ask her out on a date. My grandmother had a strict father but they were able to hang out at first as friends.

They had built a strong foundation as friends which eventually developed into a strong romance between them. Grandpa began to court my grandmother and their love for each other grew. Sometimes they would just go for a walk to spend time together. People didn't really go out to dine or eat out during those days, but they were more focused on the domestic aspect of life. They were in love and they cared deeply for one another. Eventually grandma decided that she would go and study nursing in Phoenix, Arizona at a school taught by nuns. While she was there she would write to my grandfather. Grandma had come back to visit on one of her breaks and my grandparents spent significant time together. It was hard to ignore my grandpa's persistence though, he always had that attribute. Aside from that he had piercing green eyes, white skin, and thick black curly hair that he styled with gel. All of his charm was superseded by his ability to be direct. My grandfather would get to the heart of the matter. They simply knew that they were a match made in heaven so they spoke of marriage, with an intentionality that is far to scarce today. Grandma decided to leave nursing school to be with my grandfather. When my grandma made the decision to move back they married each other at age nineteen. They had a family and were very affectionate and they always kept God and the family at the core of everything. It is a simple story that relates a simple time in a simple town. That is precisely one of my biggest takeaways from them, that they have always kept it simple and it has worked for them. My story on the other hand is a little complicated and it precisely because of this fact that I enjoy simplicity.

To understand my situation and my mom's situation, it is necessary to understand what type of upbringing she had. First understand the context in which she grew up in and then I will let you have a walk-through one of her typical days as a grade school kid in the seventies. Please keep in mind that some of the peoples' names have been altered so as to ensure their privacy is intact.

My grandparents moved around a little bit throughout Arizona, but they settled when my grandpa became a power plant supervisor. My grandma was a stay at home mom and housewife. My mother's story begins in 1967. My mother had what most would describe as an ideal childhood back in her day, though this was common for kids in her town at this time. It was still a flourishing place. Her town was still booming at the time as a direct result of the growing power plant. There are still visages of this if you were to visit today. One of the main plunders that Holbrook underwent was when the I-40 was constructed. The interstate's construction nullified the usage of the original interstate Route-66, which passed directly through Holbrook. Today the downtown area looks very well organized, but what empties this fact of its significance is that many of the buildings are abandoned or not in use today. During my mom's childhood, it was the perfect place for a new and young life. When she was first born her family was ecstatic. Mom had two lovely and hard working parents. Mom grew up in a nice, small-town, Southwestern house. She was the youngest of seven, the little princess. She received a princess' welcome from the get-go. Born into a tight-knit family which possessed deep seated Catholic roots, mom inevitably was looked out for in a special way. My aunts, her older sisters would dress her up like a doll. A visible manifestation of the harmonious home that my mother was born into. She played with her older brothers often and she would even assume some of their roles, such as wearing boy scout outfits often. She also played with their G.I. Joes frequently. All was normal and good. All was perfect.

My mom tells me of her early childhood memories, very fondly. Mom remembers that as a young elementary girl she laughed a lot with other kids. As she was growing up, mom would play outside with all of the boys and girls and her brothers. Just like the guys, she would get dirty and scrape up her knees. After a long game of hide-and-go seek and freeze-tag she would take long gulps from the garden-hose. Teachers would describe her as vivacious and cheerful. She was also a good student when she applied herself. She was just naturally intuitive. Other than flourishing at school she enjoyed life with her family at home. She played with her siblings and rode bikes in the neighborhood. Aside from the normal annoying things that siblings do to one another my uncles were very protective of her. My grandparents loved her unconditionally. She was favored by my grandparents, however this wasn't something that was envied in the household. The sentiment was mutual for everyone at home.

Then today it has become important for my mother to understand her own childhood. It became equally important for me to understand her childhood as well, to frame the suffering that followed in its proper context. Both she and my grandparents describe her childhood as ideal. Mom remembers being a decent student. She can still easily name most of the presidents as well as most bones and muscles in the human anatomy. Mom loved school and enjoyed her friends' company very much. She was a well behaved kid. She would raise her hand in class often and didn't shy away from challenges in class. Though she did struggle with remaining focused on the task at hand. When she was focused she understood the material. Her teachers would comment to grandma and grandpa that she was a very lively little girl. Even though she had a hard time concentrating she would be focused in the moment and the same applied on the playground during recess. Work hard and play hard. Grandma and Grandpa always remember mom coming home with dirty clothes from playing hard during recess. She was always in that tomboy phase. A long day of lectures, drills, quizzes, group work and all the students would be assigned homework. It was okay for her because she enjoyed it, and if it proved too difficult, her older brothers and sisters would help her with the load. School was never a chore for her and particularly not recess. She walked home every day. Daily she would stop by the local store, Pow-Wow to pick up a cool Fanta, a staple of such wonderful times. The taste of it was refreshing to her after a long day's work and a lengthy walk. Sometimes mom was accompanied by my aunts and uncles and at other times she was not. This was a routine that mom would follow religiously. It was a simple time and she was happy.

On that note, religion was one of the highest priorities for them. A frequent dinner guest was the local parish priest, Father Steven. My Uncle Steven was actually named after him. Being Catholic was a must but it wasn't to a point where any of them became robotic. My grandfather was a very involved member of the local Knights of Columbus council at the parish. This religious background was not uncommon of that region. The Latter Day Saints community, or more colloquial, the Mormons dominated the sphere. They have a large presence in the town where their stake (their version of a church building), looms over the rest of them. The Roman Catholic s follow in behind them, not by a close margin however . Mother recounts how she remembers that the two groups didn't bother each other, though the Mormons were the key players in how things in the town worked day in and day out. Maybe they were just maintaining the status quo. The Knights of Columbus conducted different fundraisers that revolved around dances and community breakfasts, while the Mormon missionaries would proselytize in town and the surrounding area. This background helps color her lifestyle and our shared secrecy throughout our lives, specifically on the matter of her sexual orientation. As a kid her joy was the most evident thing to anyone that she met. She was unaware of the rest, she only knew that she loved being alive.

Mom would share with me as I was growing up that her absolute favorite thing to do as a kid was to go camping. That was something that always stuck out to me. Her sharing her fond memories with me made me particularly appreciate camping as a kid. I understood that for her it was something that was handed on as a family tradition. It was a family event. Some of our family reunions and breakfasts were done while on a camping trip. I asked her to share with me in detail what she experienced on these trips. This is what she shared with me in her own words.

"You know Dan, camping for me was the happiest time of my childhood. Why you say? It was just so organic when I look back on it. We were together as a family and we just shared and had a good time. I was always in a tomboyish stage as a kid. I would dress up in Boy Scout uniforms and wear a football helmet. Haha, I don't even remember where I got the helmet. We played card games, we would go hiking, and have bonfires at night. The hiking would provide us with great panoramic sites of Aspen trees that were frequently caressed by the calm winds. The air was fresh and it allowed for the nice smell of the soil beneath to penetrate our nostrils. Among other great scenes I remember roasting marshmallows was a very frequent activity also, but we never did s'mores. I don't even remember knowing what that was as a kid. We weren't fancy at all but it didn't matter, we were all together. I also remember getting a new ball of some type on each trip that my dad would buy for me. I always preferred them to dolls and other girly things. I remember being fond of the family events such as cards games, board games, swimming, and hiking. I remember the smell of the wooden fire that was used to cook breakfast and the hissing of the propane tank. Those were familiar sounds, the wood crackling in the fire, I miss that from my childhood. We would have eggs, chorizo, potatoes, bacon, red chili and perfectly crisp flour tortillas that would come straight off the skillet. For lunch and dinner we would fire up the grill and have hotdogs and burgers. I also enjoyed the more personal and intimate moments that I had with my loved ones. I always had my close buddy Stretch, the very best wiener dog in the whole world. My dad would take me aside sometimes to go and catch a couple of fish. Catch and release was the method. I still remember waking up in a tent sleeping in on weekends and hearing birds chirp and feeling the cold ground underneath. My core temperature kept my blankets warm. In fact, my mom would make my little nest for me and I remember feeling comforted by that. That's a memory that still comforts me today. They were just happy times."

Something that I realized during my mother recounting her story, is that despite all of the negative things that affected us in our lives, they pale in comparison to the good experiences. Good memories can comfort us and even banish our unsettled moments, maybe even heal us.

Before things went spiraling out of control for my mom, things were good. I don't know if children do not appreciate things as deeply as adults do, however they tend to smile more than the average adult.

Maybe they are just more fully in the moment and it's because they are without so many responsibilities that they are able to enjoy these moments. Everything is more grand for them. This is not to say that it was a complete utopia, it was just normal during those days. From what she recalls, other children her age had similar experiences. It seemed untarnished, but then things weren't as good as they always seemed.

There is always more to a person than meets the eye. People have layers, and as much as we may consider them to be one dimensional, they never are. My mom had so much from her childhood that colors her personality, but one of the most significant events in her life was an extremely negative one. She was eight years old the first time that she was molested. It was a bit of a shock to her obviously. How could something like that be done to her by someone that she was supposed to trust?

He used to babysit mom only occasionally, and that's when he would take advantage and invade her. Invade is not even a word. This occurred periodically for six months. For my mom as a child, having been molested was strange for her. She didn't understand fully what had happened but she just remembers that it felt wrong and she felt scared and ashamed afterwards. Her childhood was still good, so she simply brushed things off and kept living a good life. When I reflect on her experience as she shares it with me, I cannot help but wonder what if it all had stopped there? How would have the ripples of her experience been different? How would have everything webbed out from there? Would I be here? Would the ramifications and implications be different? "I don't know," is my only answer. "I don't know," is her only answer as well. We both agreed what was, just was. This is reality and she had to move on.

Mom still flourished during school and enjoyed a lot of fun being a kid up until the sixth grade. Though, the onslaught had already begun. She had difficulty in trusting men after that, be it at school or anywhere for that matter. Mom was molested a second time. The second time was more tragic, the residual effects were more visible and they would be long lasting. It was by one of her teachers. That was one of the worst years she remembers ever having, not to discount others, because she has had some real shitty times. Later on, as an adult she tells me she found out that her former teacher had died in a car wreck. She was relieved, I suppose. "What does a kid do in that situation?", I asked mom. "Nothing, Dan. Even though I had loved ones and family, I suffered alone," was her response. She didn't tell anyone, not for a long time. I think about that though. If one reflects on that, how does a kid share the unspeakable. She didn't even know what had happened to her, but she definitely knew that it was wrong. Her strong faith in God couldn't provide her with utterance. When the time came for her to tell her parents, she could barely articulate it. Her first molester never even told her to not say anything, the fear and shame assured her silence, at least for a few years. It still wasn't any easier for her to tell me. She felt many things. Loneliness and fear. She felt it all, faceless, voiceless, unrecognized, and invaded. She had been trampled on. These are just words though, she still cannot invent any words today even to describe her experience, to describe her pain.

She carried on as best as she could and was relieved to make the transition to high school, but also scared at the same time. This tumultuous transition was not helped by her diminishing desire to excel in school. Her passion for band and drumming was growing, however these hobbies couldn't blunt the pain. Since her hobbies couldn't provide her with an avenue for relief, the easiest escape then became to hang out with the cool crowd. She had her good friends such as Susan and others, but mom would frequently drink with other kids. She also experimented heavily with marijuana. Though those peoples' faces and names have faded from her memory, she still remembers Susan really well. Even at this time mom was very fond of her. She enjoyed her companionship and attention. They would hang out a ton and they had a blast. They were best friends and that feeling was a two way street. Mutual. Though whenever Susan would share about her boyfriends, mom would feel jealous. Jealousy of this type is pretty normal for most girls at this age, so it seemed that nothing should be made of it. In retrospect mom tells me that she remembers being talented enough to go to a university on a drumming or band scholarship. She never fulfilled this potential but her life took a different turn. Susan and mom weren't really thinking along these lines though. "I just wasn't that together at that time in my life," she shared with me. She eventually got a senior position at the local bank and my grandparents were so proud of her. However, this was short-lived, and they were very disappointed when she let them know of her plans to move away. The fact that she didn't go to college and that she left her job, wouldn't dampen her adventurous spirit. Mom and I have always had adversity but this is something that we share, we are spontaneous and adventurous.

Right after high school both mom and Susan decided to move to Minnesota. Susan had her brother and sister living there and since they both, mom and her friend, weren't going to college they decided to embark on another type of adventure. Once settled in Minneapolis they began working a nine to five job each. They would hang out on weekends and enjoyed each other's companionship. It seemed ideal for a recent high school graduate. Some of mom's older habits followed her as well. The legal drinking age in Minnesota was eighteen at the time so they naturally took advantage and indulged themselves. Another novelty was that mom then experienced her first baseball game. It was a Twins game. She began to become more aware of what was happening around her with all of the new excitement that she was discovering, but she also became more introspective. Increasingly mom and Susan grew to a bit more co-dependent on each other. Drinking legally and the baseball games weren't the only new things to my mom, she was being shaped into the person she would become for the next several years.

My mother developing feelings for Susan was also newfound, which may have resulted in part because of mom's co-dependency. This attraction was organic though. There wasn't a sudden moment where mom realized it, it was only later on that it dawned on her.

"I don't know when my friendship and longing for Susan's attention evolved into something more. I was always attracted to her as a friend and we just clicked from the beginning. Looking back though, I did feel differently towards her, than I did my other female friends. This began before we moved to Minnesota."

Unlike their friendship, this feeling was not shared. Susan didn't view my mom in that way at all. Susan was oblivious to the fact that my mom had a crush on her. My mom still remembers being jealous of Susan's boyfriends and other lady friends whenever they spoke or hung out during high school. Mom felt like this for a period of one year or so. Throughout this entire year mom carried on with this unexpressed affection. "I love you, or I like you. Those words that I never told her," she tells me today. Once again we have those unspeakable and unspoken words. Hindsight vision is always twenty-twenty, pristine. Mom remembers knowing that she liked Susan but she wasn't really aware of it at the time, now she knows clearly that particular attraction was romantic. So at the time the words couldn't be expressed because she didn't even know where she stood with it. She only lived with Susan for a year and then decided to seek something familiar again. She missed home and she would be moving back.

She eventually made it back to Arizona and settled into an apartment and job. My grandparents had moved out of town, so she lived with an uncle before she started 'adulting' hardcore. Working full-time at a Safeway was pretty monotonous for her at first but she was sticking to it to be able to keep up her bills and payments. It was during this time that she felt a longing to return to her hometown. When she moved back, she opened up to my parents about her past. She let them know of what happened to her as a sixth grader. They spoke to the superintendent about what had transpired. A police officer was present from the local department. She didn't find the justice she hoped for. Painfully, she retells everything that happened on that terrible day,

"As I informed the superintendent about everything the police officer was there and so were my parents. Mom and Dad were really hurt, obviously. Due to some technicality on statute of limitations they weren't able to make a formal case to the local law enforcement, but however my parents attempted to make a case to have his teaching certification revoked. I travelled to Phoenix to testify to the school board of education. He had pictures of me, from the annual of when I was a sixth grader as a part of his defense. He and others were putting me down, and they tried to shame me, stating that he wouldn't denigrate himself to be with a kid like me. They were successful. Nonetheless, I told them all that had happened to no avail. They voted to keep him in. I am over it now but I still view child molesters as grotesque."

She will always view child molesters with an eye of pity and confusion, and this is good. It is good to forgive, but not to forget.

Sometime after my mom's revelation, she wanted to attempt suicide and end it quickly. Inside she begged for justice, and this was never satisfied for her. She also held the unanswered question of, why? "Why did this happen to me?", she still goes with this question unanswered. Mom is grateful every day because she didn't execute her plan to take her own life.. My mom knows what if feels like to have an overbearing weight of shame on her shoulders, and if the way out for her was death, she would have gladly taken it. It is more than being caught in rock and a hard place to possess this feeling, or to be possessed by the feeling itself. Some are so possessed by such a stifling sentiment that the only logical option for them is to end life in this world. It is a unique experience to consider ending it all on this earth without much consideration of what is next, if the eternal is even a forethought. It is completely another thing to follow through with ending it here, though mom and I never were pushed that far. Mom wasn't the slow destructive type to perform self-harm intentionally, but she did have bad habits that lingered for years.

Her life mainly consisted of playing the drums in a band and going out with friends and working. Her hobby was what helped sustain her for a while. During this time she never had any intimate or serious relationships but at the age of twenty-four, lighting strikes. She did something that she didn't think that she could be capable of again, she met a man and trusted him.

She first met him at the Safeway where she was working. "Our eyes locked and whatever task I was doing seemed unimportant,"

Mom reminisces. Sergio was his name. His name wasn't all too common nor did he seem like a common man. He captivated her. It was later though that, at a mutual friend's wedding, she saw him again. He was handsome, with a stocky build, fly, and charming. He had nice eyes and was a smooth talker, so much so that his words could entrance you. She had never viewed a man as beautiful as this one before. They danced the night away. He mesmerized her. Mom says that he instilled trust in her, that he made her feel safe. This was a feeling that she had not experienced with another man aside from her father. Pretty soon they dated and the emotions were running strong. They would see each other frequently and things were moving fast. Soon after having met, within that first month of what was supposed to be forever, they were intimate with one another. He was her first real love. It was all supposed to last forever. Soon thereafter she was pregnant. Once mom let him know, he was shocked and excited to hear the news. Please keep in mind, that he was telling her that he would marry her, and that he would work to support her and their eventual family. She thought he was the one. I understand now that a person in her circumstance would be very bold to trust a person with everything, especially because of her minimal dating experience and background. The next morning he was gone. Then the following day she didn't hear from him, nor the next. Eventually it was a week gone by and she heard nothing of him. The funny thing is that she was intimate with him only once and that was what it took. There she sat alone and afraid of what the future would hold. She was twenty-four, pregnant, and confused of whom she could trust. Most 'religious' people in town wouldn't willingly extend a helping hand, of any sort. These were seemingly insurmountable obstacles. This was a more than difficult situation for mom. She was pregnant and husbandless. I hadn't even been born yet, and I was already fatherless. These weren't only my mom's set of ugly circumstances, I didn't ask for life on this earth but this was now our set of ugly circumstance

CHAPTER 2
MOM ARE YOU GAY?

Despite the circumstances, grandmother was excited at having a new baby grandson. On the other hand, Grandpa was very disappointed at how my mother's romantic relationship unfolded, he took it pretty hard at first. The next day though he mellowed out and came around, nothing could be given except love and support. He understood that it was an emotional and spiritual crime for my biological father to have abandoned us in that situation, and as the son, I didn't deserve any of the punishment for it.

Mom wasn't alone but she felt that way. Sometimes feelings run together and they become enmeshed, she felt alone because she felt scared and vice versa. Many people supported my mom during the pregnancy, and though they helped her along, this was mom's journey, which had now become mine. My aunt Zena, by marriage to my uncle, was very supportive of my mother during the pregnancy. My aunt would accompany my mother to lamaze classes so that she could prepare for the labor process. "It was nice to have that comfort," mother recounts. Mom's good friend, Gertrude Sawyer, would frequently get ice cream with her and eat other spontaneous cravings. Gertrude was also pregnant at the time but a bit further along. After my birth, both I and Gertrude's boy, were baptized on the same day at Our Lady of Guadalupe Parish. All of this support was helpful in a practical sense yes, but that sense of comfort that my mother craved emotionally would only come when she felt me moving inside. My mother worked during the entire pregnancy up until two months before my birth. All of this was happening, the ebb and flow of each day's work, but my mother says it was a good and healthy pregnancy. At times it seemed so fast to her.

In the fall of 1991 I was born in Show Low, Arizona. It was one of those cherished memories that she holds dear in her heart. Mom tells me the story,

"The day that my son was born, I was scared, excited, and apprehensive of my future. My first baby, my first responsibility. When my water broke, I knew it was happening. My mom helped drive me to the doctor's office Dr. Gordon. I felt like I had the flu and I was in extreme pain. We arrived at the hospital. My mom, dad, Zena were all there. My sister, Mary and her boys, arrived right after Dan was born. When my son was born, another part of me emerged. The mama bear, my instincts as a mother awoke. He just looked at me with pure love, and I him."

That was the beginning of everything for me. Initially my mother was going to name me Gregory Emilio after my grandma and my grandpa's brother respectively, Gregoria and Emilio, but it didn't seem right to her. When I was born she just felt that Daniel was right for me. My grandparents extended to me the same treatment that my mother received at her birth. Since mom always enjoyed my grandparents favor, so did I. After I was born we went to Pinetop-Lakeside, Arizona. My grandparents lived there so mom decided that a visit with them would be nice. We stayed there a month. The day after I was born we went to see them, they had a breakfast for us, and since my father was not there, my grandma stepped up to fill in. By all appearances I was going to have tremendous support from everyone in my family. To a certain degree I enjoyed my family's support throughout my life and in many instances throughout, that support and understanding would be lacking. My mom found that current situation there to be wanting so a change became necessary for her.

After our month visit there my mother and I moved to Holbrook to live for the next four years. Mom was very playful with me, she would make me laugh a lot. It was hard not to play with me, I was a cute and chubby toddler, perfect for everyone to pinch my cheeks. I think once the newness of having a kid, and the responsibilities had set in and were outweighing the fun to be had, my mom began to have a shift. My mother felt alone at this time even though she had me. She was basically a kid who had a kid. She worked often and had several different sitters take care of me throughout her week at work and on some weekends as well. She was still involved in a band and she would have different gigs at bars and other small venues. All the while I was just growing fast and discovering things. I was a happy toddler, but mom was heading down a dark road led by confusion. She was often sad during the pregnancy, and particularly after my birth because she wanted for me to have a father. That is when the lack of an immediate male figure became most apparent to her. She felt guilty for this, for bringing a child in the world where he wouldn't have a father. She resorted to old ways of coping that weren't so healthy.

Old habits die hard, and when they return it is typically with a vengeance. The incentive of having a healthy pregnancy wasn't there anymore. There should have been an incentive for having a healthy lifestyle and home, for her sake and for my own. She mainly smoked weed with her coworkers but she would sometimes use hardcore drugs with her fellow band members. The band was called High Lonesome, and mom was the drummer. The band name seems appropriate for this stage in her life, high and lonesome she was. It reminds me of a song that was released two years after my birth, Keep Ya Head Up, by Tupac Shakur. "I know that it's kind of rough and you're feelin all alone, daddy's long gone and he left you by your lonesome." The song gets brighter and it has a positive message of encouragement, but my mother didn't get the memo. She had only distractions that didn't bring any solutions. With the band crowd my mother experimented with cocaine and meth. I wonder what the band could have been like if they didn't use drugs. I wonder how my mother would have taken a different path. It is no use to wonder, it didn't play out this way. In any case the band probably didn't have a shot since early on they were more focused on partying and drugs. To state the obvious, mom didn't have healthy methods or outlets to deal with the obstacles in her life. Our situation could only worsen from thereon with this negativity.

Then things worsened. What really propelled her meth addiction was she became pregnant with a second child. This was when I was two years old. My mother had met a guy at work and they became intimate. It was more so just a hook up phase, mom still battled with trust issues, but it is ironic that she could give herself in this way without truly giving herself to another person. She never told him that she was pregnant, neither did she tell him about the abortion. She didn't want to bring another kid into the world, nor did she feel ready to do so. Mom's parents were deeply Catholic so their stance would be pretty loud about abortion aside from that she wasn't really serious with the guy. Mom felt like she was out of options. Her friend Cassie urged her in the choice to abort the baby. My mother tells me that she was deeply wounded at this time, "I felt that after the abortion I was stripped of my womanhood, stripped of my femininity. I killed a baby." As a result my mom began to use more heavily. She kept her silence on this matter for a long time. She had deep pain in her life and when this truth about her was revealed to me, it made a lot of sense as to why she had such emotional trauma. Mom told me this while I was in seminary. I was one of very few people that knew about the abortion. If you are reading this now, then the silence has definitely been broken and now this information is public. This was fact that I learned during my early twenties and it was a shock to me. If this was my internal feeling about it, I could only imagine what my mother had endured. Yes the silence has been broken, not for the sake of wearing my heart on my sleeve, it's so that others can learn from these experiences.

Certainly there are lessons shared in my mom's story, in our story. The abortion tore her up so much that she needed some sort of escape from her pain. She had some hardships so far, and some were self-inflicted. Her meth addiction became so bad that she had to consider entering a rehab center. My aunt Margaret was the first one to bring up this option to my mom. She was the one that expressed this concern most forcefully and this helped my mom to go in the first place. She came to her senses. It was here that she began to turn things around for us, but only briefly. Mom did go to a rehab center for a brief stint and that was enough to get her back on track, I was enough to get her back on track. One truism that she learned from the center was in order to change your habits, you have to change your playground. She took this advice to heart, she felt a transition was necessary.

At this stage I was four years old and mom wanted to me to have a good life, so in an effort to avoid this bad scene mom moved us back to where my grandparents were at. We were back in Pinetop-Lakeside, maybe a permanent move my mother hoped. My grandparents' influence on me was and has been impactful, even to today. They have always had a strong work ethic. They helped raise me, and they always tried very hard to get their character strengths to stick with me. Some of their strengths include service, kindness, true beauty, warmth, and charity. I am not idolizing them, but I cannot deny that they are the prime example that comes to my mind when I think of a perfect couple. When we first moved back to my grandparents' home, they were unaware of the my mom's second pregnancy and the abortion all together. They actually do not know of it, to this day. It is a curious thing to keep secrets under wraps from the closest loved ones we have, especially if they have a right to know the truth. It is still a more curious thing when the truth is concealed from you. There is such a thing as private life and we all have our own right to that because it is healthy. Meanwhile, there is secrecy, and only egotism and conceitedness are fed with this one. I have had my fair share of both in life, and though one is negative, it doesn't mean that we cannot grow from our experiences.

This is a common theme throughout my life as a child, secrecy and lies. It wasn't all too common in my earlier years, however it was present for sure. I think that a lie could be characterized by the following three ways: to tell an outright lie, to tell a half-truth, and to refrain from telling the truth to those who deserve to know it, which is silence when the truth is warranted. The complete silence is the least frequent of these. I felt as if I had to find a way to wiggle around one major reality in my life but this trickled to other aspects of my personality. More on this in a bit. It was not until later on that I felt the necessity to lie about my life for a number of reasons. I had much to learn.

In the meantime, I found myself back in Pinetop-Lakeside. They were small towns and they were homey in many ways. I remember most of the time I would stay with my grandparents at their home in the local country club. They practically raised me. My mother worked often at Safeway so I would spend my time away from school with my grandparents. Some of the seeds my grandparents planted in me I have yet to see bud into something that I will be proud of in my life, but they planted them and I need to keep cultivating them. They are sort of underlying principles for me. They taught me the Catholic faith, they were simple people, and they always led by example. I do know that grandma and grandpa definitely helped deepen the sense of wonderment in me that children naturally possess. At their home I had to be disciplined. I remember waking up on some weekends and my grandparents had some sort of chore for me to do after breakfast. Now don't get the wrong idea, they were retired at this point and sometimes retirees are some of the busiest and hardest working people out there, but these chores we did alongside each other. Grandma would have me garden and plant flowers. I wouldn't cook but I would sometimes be asked to offer a helping hand. Sometimes I would begrudgingly do this task, but I would prefer to just set the table. Since I was a young kid, and a bit of a loner at times, it helped to have things to do, which would keep me preoccupied. I was a loner, yes, but I was naturally outgoing, and I loved meeting new people. I didn't shy away from meeting new people. Actually the contrary, I was outgoing and I made friends relatively easy. This was something that was apparent when I would go to church with my grandparents. My mother didn't go to Sunday Mass anymore, so I went with grandma and grandpa. The encouraged me to grow at church. They have made all the difference in my life, and I would know it for a longtime, but the faith would as well.

I began altar serving at an early age. So then began my activity in the Catholic Church. I remember loving the feeling that I got serving Mass, and that was a sense of service that my grandparents helped foster in me. I remember kneeling at the sanctuary ready to ring-aling those bells. To this day the smell of incense evokes many memories for me. I was like a trained German shepherd ready to go at the priest's signal. I would also frequently help set up for CCD, or Catholic catechism as it was commonly known. I saw many familiar faces from school there, some of them eager to learn and other's came just for the free Little Caesar's pizza. I was a little bit of both sides of the equation. Whatever the situation, we all chowed-down during class. It was actually here that I had my first crush. Her name was Julie Duncan, or JD for short. I was lucky if I could help hand out boxed-juices, so I could personally hand one to her. These outward activities brought me peace. Peace being a still and mainly interior activity. It almost made me forget how absent my mother was from my life at the time. It was difficult, and I noticed her absence but I knew that things were still fine. Sometimes we lose peace, but it is something that can be regained if we revisit some old habits.

Sometimes the tasks gave me purpose. My grandfather was a long time Knights of Columbus member and whenever they sponsored food drives or other service projects, I was his little captain and go to guy. Together we would mow the parish lawn almost every week. The Knights of Columbus had spoken with the parish priest and they began the project of building a columbarium. A columbarium is where the cremation ashes from deceased parishioners are kept as a final resting place. Together, my grandfather and I, and the rest of the knights helped build the columbarium for the parish. He was always about giving back. My grandfather did his best to instill in me an attitude of service. One vivid memory that I reflect on occasionally is when we would go to a shelter run by nuns in New Mexico. The nuns had set up a home for unwedded mothers who were otherwise unable to have enough stability to bring their pregnancies to full term. It was during the summer, and we would make the five hour trip to spend a week helping out with various construction and service projects. One year we even built a brick wall for the security of the facility. I thought it was a neat spot, and I had a blast doing fun things outside, all the while grandpa and his friends were busy working. Since grandpa was my only father figure, I looked up to him a lot. He exuded confidence and was a strong man, a man simply sure of himself. I wanted to be like him. I am special to my grandparents and they are special to me. They taught me to pray in good times and bad ones. I thought that maybe I could pray so that bad things and bad times wouldn't happen. Once I even prayed that my grandparents would never die. I never had a dad, I didn't have siblings, and my mom was fun, but I never really felt that she expressed her love to me. Other than having my grandparents, I felt alone. I had a fear that I may lose them one day. The hope that they would remain with me forever was probably the most sincere I had up to that point. Their impact on my life has been great to say the least. Their mark on my childhood is indelible.

When I was a kid they enjoyed the fact that I would entertain the idea of the priesthood. They even made me a little Mass setup so that I could practice. Everyone at the parish knew me, and some of them probably even wondered if I would be a priest one day. I was just that kid. Grandpa had frequent guests over at his place who were men of similar age. They would share stories with each other about their youth and the like. Most of them are retirees, among whom were doctors, pediatricians, and engineers. My grandparents lived in the country club and they had many things to do. They had a recreation center and the golf course which was fun to hang out at. My grandpa and I would golf, and he would even let me drive the golf-cart, although I almost flipped the golf-cart a few times. We would look at each other and smirk as if we didn't notice what just happened. They were simple times and we lived simply. My grandparents radiated that simplicity. They always had zero guile in conversation. My grandparents never let their surroundings get to their head, their humble beginnings made them very grounded people.

Both of my grandparents were very close to me. They are still close to me. My grandfather was like my father. We had a lot of memories together. When I was a child, grandpa and grandma would take me out to the woods every now and again and we would chop a tree down. I would help as much as loading the truck bed so we could have wood for fires during the wintertime. It was a cool experience to be in nature with my grandparents, there were no distractions or crazy external stimulants, it was just the three of us working together. When we would take a break we would chow down on some delicious sandwiches that my grandma would pack us. It was perfect.

Another fond memory that I still hold closely, occurred when I was in the fifth grade. Grandpa took me to a Phoenix Suns vs. L.A. Clippers game. He got some expensive tickets from a friend of his, "for my grandson and I", he said. I remember it so vividly. My mom purchased her tickets separately and came with us. These were awesome seats. It was the fact that grandpa knew that I was such a big basketball fan that made this all the more special. We arrived to the game early to take our seats in the fifth row in the very middle. I went to see the players practice and a security guard noticed me and asked if I wanted to be a security kid. I didn't know what that was but it sounded cool enough to do. He waved my mom down and asked if I could hang out and be a security kid. She answered that it was fine for me to go along. He took me through the tunnel where the players come through before the game begins. He showed me around and gave me a security kid shirt. The security guard gave another kid and I instructions on how to be intimidating and how to 'make sure that the situation was secure.' When I first saw the players I couldn't believe how tall they were. They were all huge. We watched the game from the floor and no experience can replace it. I was so into basketball and as a result, I was mesmerized. Shawn Marion, Amar'e Stoudemire, and a few other notable guys were killing it. When halftime swung around I was eating the same food that the players were eating. The Suns won so I was feeling just as victorious as they were. My mom bought me a ball and all of the players signed it before they went home. It was a surreal experience, to say the least. I felt starstruck and my grandpa was the one who made this all possible for me. I will always cherish this memory. My grandpa and grandma are simple people but they have always made magic happen in my life. They were always down to earth and when I was with them I had peace. It was an interesting contrast to what life was like with my mother whenever we were on our own.

Whenever I was at mom's place, my world seemed to be in constant flux. Things in life rarely seemed settled. People often times speak of how difficult it is to be a single mother in our day. Still often, many others forget how much of an impact this can hold on a kid. Mom wasn't around much so I had to feed myself, as can be imagined, my eating habits weren't very nourishing. I had TV dinners on some occasions, but I mainly ate crackers and cheese and bologna sandwiches. Countless times I would open the refrigerator to peek in only to walk away disappointed by what was in there. Rarely did I have a home cooked meal and if I did, it had a dismal taste. Now I am not playing the victim because my mom and I both had our fair share of ugly in life, and so does everyone else. I would ask God why he rejected me? I asked of him why was it that my mom didn't love me? Similar to my mom, I began to discover early on in my childhood that life isn't always a sweet ride.

I longed for the idea of having a father, but that was never something that my mom and I spoke about. Something was missing and it would become apparent to me why. Mom had not shared with my grandparents that she was lesbian though they had suspected it. My mother began seeing a woman romantically while I was early on in elementary school. Her name was Angelina Wilson. She was my mother's first open same-sex relationship, but it took time before my mom shared this with my grandparents. At first neither mom nor Angelina knew of the other's orientation. They were just acquainted because they both worked at a Safeway. Mom worked in town, and

Angelina in a neighboring town's Safeway. Angelina was originally from California somewhere. I still wonder what their initial conversation was like. "There wasn't anything particular about Angelina that struck me at first, I just knew that she was friendly," says my mother. Mom liked how much of a fun personality she had. She was an outdoorsy kind of person. She was pretty outgoing, she enjoyed going to the movies. They would hang out because they had some sort of a single mom bond. Angelina didn't have any children on her own. This is why Mom also liked the fact that Angelina had adopted her four nieces and nephews, and she was raising them on her own. The children came from a messy situation. Their dad had molested one of the girls and he caught wind that the authorities we going to be informed of this. He killed his wife and then committed suicide on Easter day. Messy situation is an understatement. If I was only beginning my rough path, what the hell did these kids make of their lives? In any case, my mother thought that this was a magnanimous move on her part and she admired her for it. It seemed a selfless act.

Eventually something sparked between her and my mom. I didn't really know what was happening between them. The kids were all older than me. It was a cool match I thought. Sometimes we all, mom, Angelina, I, and the others would make trips to Phoenix and check out the zoo and other sites. The kids were always hanging out with me, and I with them. My mom had a new friend, I thought it seemed okay.

The other children and I were somewhat dissimilar from each other but we made it work. My mother always made sure that I was always well kept and that I minded my manners. They had issues with misconduct in almost any setting. The oldest was Matthew and he would get into trouble at school sometimes. I remember feeling bad because he was genuinely a nice guy to me. He would look out for me. I remember hanging out over at their place and Matthew would sometimes make me a plate to eat after our little excursions through the woods. The other three were Leah, Noah, and Ruby. They all liked me from the beginning with the exception of Ruby. She would often times direct her snarky comments to me pretty sharply. She had trouble accepting me because my personality overshadowed hers. It wasn't my fault that I was outgoing, cheerful, and talkative. Maybe since they were so close in age also underlined why she was mean to me. They were all older than me but Ruby was closest to me in age. I guess I stole her spotlight a little, Angelina liked me and so did the guys. I made a good impression on them, I was always a natural kid up to this point in my life. My mom says, "You were like a little adult, you did the right thing at the right time. You were always well behaved." The secrecy settled in later. I never realized that my mom was lesbian and my seven year old mind believed that Angelina and mom were just good friends. I had just gotten back from riding bikes with the boys one day and I decided that I would just hang out at their home to watch tv with Ruby. We were sitting on the bed watching an episode of Hey Arnold. It was a back to back day for the show on Nickelodeon, and the next episode was about to start. She didn't change the channel during commercials so I was thinking of something to say during the commercials. I remember trying my best to express to her how much I was glad that our parents were friends and as a result we had all become friends with each other.

"No dummy, they're not friends," Ruby said.

"What do you mean?" I questioned her.

"They're gay, they're not friends," she retorted so matter-of-factly.

I was like, "Whaaat!" My heart sank when I heard this.

I remember getting up and pacing back and forth in front of the bathroom door. I was confused and a little heated. I couldn't have even of imagined that. "My mom is gay?" I asked myself. I couldn't be sure until I asked her. I waited by the window in anticipation for my mother to arrive so I could find out. She pulled up in her little black S-10 truck as I was feeling frustrated. I didn't even finish the episode of Hey Arnold. "How would I initiate this conversation?" I thought to myself. I stepped into the truck and I was looking out the window quietly as if really fixing my gaze on something, but I was still just wondering how to ask my question.

"Mom are you gay?" I finally asked her.

She was quiet for a little while and she answered, "Yes Dan," in the same matter of fact manner in which Ruby had told me.

I was frozen. I didn't want that to be true. It was with that same surety that Candice had said it, I remember. I also remember that I felt bad the rest of the ride home. My world was coming to an end, the prospect of me having a dad one day had disappeared. It was a moment of realness that my mother had with me that kind of shattered me. I was hoping that I could have a dad one day soon. My initial thought was, "What the heck! My mom is gay! What does this mean for me?" It was unspoken but mom and I would not touch this subject with a ten-foot pole. We never talked about sexuality between couples at all, much less homosexuality. I don't think many people touch on this subject with their children and I wonder how this dynamic was supposed to have worked in my own life? I was left to fend for myself in this aspect of my life, along with many other aspects.

Now that I look back, if I had never found this out about her then, I would still wonder why a person like her could not manage to tie down some hunk of a man. She had a great smile and beautiful olive skin. She was petite, of delicate frame, and supple. She was also nice and caring. She is still to this day a great gift-giver. Once she surprised me on my birthday with a Mongoose bike with front and rear pegs, but one year she topped that when she rented a hotel suite with a playroom for my friends and I to enjoy. We ate well on that occasion, and I was really surprised. If she could make me feel this happy then she could certainly make a man happy. That was the last piece to my puzzle, at least that was the conception in my mind. That was just how it was supposed to work. I was back in this S-10 truck on that devastating day and I didn't mention it to her for a long time, nor did she to me. On this subject, there was only silence.

I didn't realize that at the time how much the question, "Where's your dad?" would warrant a response. Though I buried that hope deep down inside, externally it would rise from its shallow grave. Whenever the question would come up I would find a way to flat out lie about it. Not that any other kids merited a response but I didn't think about it in those terms. If the other kids would ask where my dad was at, I would say that mom had divorced my dad. Sometimes I would say that she was seeing somebody at the moment, that's the half-truth. She was seeing someone, it definitely wasn't a man. I never said who this was of course. I felt so ashamed to even admit it to myself.

What's more, Angelina's adopted kids were very badly behaved, I couldn't say we were like family because I didn't really accept that. Those kids and I, like many others in the world, come from crappy situations that we have no control over. There we have common ground. I suppose that I didn't consider this at the time. I didn't consider many other people much beyond a superficial level. I was preoccupied with my current situation.

Other times I was just aloof and forgetful. I would frequently forget about my mom's orientation or just tried to flat out block it from my mind. I must have really tried that much more to forget when I would hang around Angelina's kids or whenever I saw Angelina. The recurring question from the other kids, "where's your dad?", would pop up whenever I was not expecting it, though after I while I was able to acquire a sense of when it would come my way. I was quick on my feet. One lie that I would say is one that I used in the following instance, is of when a school friend of mine's mother wanted to introduce her brother to my mom. His mother had the hope that something could be kindled between them. I told her that my mom was dating an FBI agent. I never realized how inflated like a balloon that caricature of a lie was, it couldn't be real, huh? Very inflated was my desire to fit in though. I don't know if it was my ego yet, because I was a kid who only wanted to fit in. In my mind, the more I blew the lie up the more credible it would be. This had to be my solution, to create a Dan that I thought others would accept. It was a faulty solution, but it worked at the time.

I didn't have a solution for finding this missing puzzle piece aside from hoping that my mom would become straight. It was painful to want the companionship of a father and to not have that need be met. Unmet needs can inspire sadness, anger, and resentment. It can take years to build this up and years to get rid of it as well. One instance, that I remember as a kid which made me long for a father, was when I was at Wal-Mart with my mom. I went to an aisle to pick out a toy. There, I saw a father get down on one knee and hand a toy to his young son. The kid's face radiated as he smiled and hugged his dad. I wanted that companionship, but my dad had abandoned us. My mom or grandparents didn't let me know this, but I had assumed that this was true. I wasn't wrong. At this moment I had to accept that I didn't have a dad, that I may never have a dad. I was angry at my dad and at God for having rejected me. Merely silence, what could be done? I had to live my life. This was the first time that I felt bad about my relationship with God.

This lack of resolution would build up in me whenever I lied about this specific topic, but it began to spread to other areas in my life, areas where I felt like I wasn't enough. This void began to spread where I felt that my life with my mother wasn't enough. I wish that I realized how really awesome of a mother I had in other respects. She had her faults but each time has its own merit, each time has its own goodness and though these were the beginnings of a rough path, my mom was a spectacular person. It took a lot of time and a lot of retrospection to realize this. In my younger days I realized I couldn't control who my mom was or better yet her life choices, so I had to focus on what I could control, salvaging my image.

Soon I was able to create myself to be whoever I wanted to be. I began to lie about my academics. I now know that a person doesn't have to be the smartest to have good intuition. Often times being a bookworm doesn't equate with a wise person or even just someone who is intelligent. I continued to inflate the caricatured version of myself. If I was hanging out with the smarter kids and the kids from well to do families, I would pretend to be smarter than what I really was. I lied more than once that I was formerly in the gifted program. No one challenged me on my claim, but I felt like I had to nail this, in order to impress others. Nailed it. If someone had challenged me on my claims my reply would be, "Oh, well I was asked to join the gifted program but I turned it down." As if I could take it or leave it! Ha! This got even worse and I would lie gratuitously. I told my fifth grade teacher that my mother and I made a trip to Notre Dame to watch a football game, even though really, my grandparents and I are great fans. It was more so a fabrication of my imagination though I did have plenty of Notre Dame stimulation. My room was decked out with all things Notre Dame. I had a Notre Dame throw rug, customized comforter, my clock was Notre Dame and so was my trashcan. My aunt, also my baptismal godmother, once gave me a Notre Dame mug that I still proudly own today. My favorite movie to watch and re-watch was Rudy, a simple classic. My teacher believed me simply because I could assert a lie so convincingly. It wasn't so much that I could tell a great story or even a story really well that I knew when I had them, it was just a look in their face that let me know they believed me. That look brought relief. If life was so simple, we make fables and stories and they become reality but this isn't so. Lying was my escape.

It became very important for me to tell what ever lie, half-truth, or even a complete truth, whenever convenient, in order to fit in. All of my friends were church going people, Mormons and Catholics, so I was afraid of rejection. During this entire time Angelina and her kids went to the same parish as my grandparents and I did. We still hung out a ton but I preferred the well to do crowd, the athletic kids, the smart ones, the affluent, and the religious. Still, I liked most kids and I could make friends easily. It was harder to hang out with the influential group because I had to force myself to keep up appearances with them. I 'had' to fit in. I could have hung out with the Goth or Emo kids or some of the other kids at the trailer park and I would have been accepted more for who I was. They would have considered my mother's situation much less. I am not passing judgement on this group of kids. Please don't misinterpret this to mean that I still wasn't myself, I just wanted to be accepted. Most children are fully themselves in the moment, but this type of naturalness and innocence can be robbed by different circumstances, as I have discovered for myself. It is also around this age that the affective filter begins to kick in. I still carried my naturalness but it was hindered because I felt on guard. I was naturally a person of service and I loved making new friends but I needed that extra piece of the puzzle to be complete. A puzzle, in my mind, was easy to draw this analogy. I obviously didn't have to lie about this topic so long as this topic wasn't brought up, Matthew, Leah, Noah, and Ruby already knew the truth about me. As a result I was at ease with them. They knew that I didn't have a dad but they didn't know how much I longed for an old man of my own. I can't single myself out, I am sure they longed for the same affirmation that I so desperately needed. Mom didn't know my longing either, I perceived. I couldn't know her heart. She had me in her life, I wasn't enough for her. It was rough to split the one person in my life that was meant to be there for me, I mean she gave birth to me. There was nothing particularly bad about Angelina, she was always nice and loving and I got along well with her adopted kids. Matthew was especially nice to me. Matthew, if you are reading this, thank you for being there for me you were like a brother to me. Mom chose to have Angelina in her life, so I had to share her.

My mother sought companionship like I longed to have a Dad. My mother had a friend throughout this period, who was also a lesbian. Her name was Dawn McCormick. She was so nice and good to me. She loved hiking. She taught me how to shoot a gun. Even though I strived to block my mom's sexuality from my mind I never picked up on the fact that Dawn was also lesbian. I just never sensed that vibe between mom and her. There was nothing like the vibe that I sensed between Angelina and mom. Mom had not yet shared this with my grandparents. Though that was something that my grandparents had already caught wind of, but they never said anything. My mother eventually decided to come out and tell my grandparents that she was a lesbian. They had suspected this for a while already because my mom was always hanging out with Angelina however, they were disappointed to hear this in my mom's own words. Mom also felt their disappointment. They didn't take the news nowhere near as hard as the rest of my family did. My family used to have a neat tradition where my grandparents would convene with my aunts and uncles and speak freely about family matters. This was one of those times that my family thought it was necessary to have a meeting. Some family members expressed that they didn't want my mom's partner around them or their children. In any case, mom and Angelina began to see each other, and since Angelina was becoming a bigger part in my mom's life, she undoubtedly had to become a part of my life, whether I wanted it or not.

During this stage my mother was getting more into using angel reading cards. They are similar to Tarot cards. She would visit psychics who would tell my mom's future. I thought it was all bullshit. One of the psychics had her psychology degree hanging on the wall. That lady was way off on everything, and I knew for sure that it was bullshit. She was good at reading people's body language, soothsaying, and tickling ears to make people feel better, and that was about the extent of her talents. Most of them also believed in reincarnation. They would relate my mom's present life to her 'past' life in an attempt to draw parallels, but they did it in such a general way so that it could seem credible. They also attempted to reconcile the present life with her 'future' life happenings. I wasn't convinced on their reasoning for why my mom was single. My mom believed heavily in reincarnation, and this is how she also tried to explain our lives. How convenient for them. Many of them played on her belief to state that she had limited control as to how to steer our lives. She believed that we were paying for things in this life because of how we lived our past lives. You can tell that I am a skeptic. I didn't know if reincarnation was real at the time but I definitely knew that it was one-hundred percent against Catholic teaching, so I rejected it. There was always something weird about the occult. My mom once performed a Wiccan ritual or some sort of witchcraft with incense at our home and it freaked me out. Immediately I knew something was wrong. I can think of better times. It still gives me frightening chills to think of. I think at one point she was having psychics try to influence the cosmos so that she could have a good partner or in order for her to keep Angelina her life. Ironically enough, she ended her five year relationship with Angelina because she found out that Angelina had cheated on her in the second year of them dating. It was a relief to me that she was able to walk away.

Obviously not everything throughout my childhood experience with mom was negative, I had many positive experiences as well. One weekly quality time that I would get with mom was when we would go to the Movie Dome to pick out and rent movies. We would watch them during the weekend and then we would take them back. This was a constant during my childhood and at these times I felt fortunate. At other times I was not so fortunate.

Sometime after mom became involved with another woman named Tammy. Their relationship didn't last a long time. She lived nearby and she had three girls. She had a decent personality, but her children also proved to be a handful. One of the girls dropped out of school, and another one of them ended up in jail for any number of drug related crimes, and the last one was close to my age. Tammy drove a battered vehicle. I would always fear that it would crap out on her whenever she turned corners. Anyway, Tammy told me once that I would be a businessman one day. Yet to be fulfilled.

In those days, I didn't worry about visiting other places and enjoying site-seeing. I was still content to enjoy the simple things in life, like family and friendships. My daily life was simple. First thing in the morning I would turn the TV on and switch the channel to either MTV or VH1. It was good to have some background noise while I got ready. When I had enough time to sit down, I would work on the previous night's homework if necessary, otherwise I would flip between MTV's AMTV and VH1's Top 20 Countdown. I was flipping between two channels to avoid commercials or to catch the hottest video, and cranking out my math assignment due for the day. Right before the bus would arrive I would stuff my assignment into my backpack. I would head outside and begin my day.

I remember riding the bus to school every day and I would always notice this enormous house on my way there. I remember wanting to go inside and see it. One day a kid was getting on the bus but I didn't speak to him nor he to me. I just wondered who he was and what his parents did. We met the coming summer at basketball camp called Hot Shots. I don't really remember how it happened to the exact detail but the moment was as spontaneous as they come.

It was mid-June when the basketball camp started. I met Blake while we were doing basketball drills. I hated those things. At one point I fell behind him and a couple of others during the suicide repetitions. Once he had passed me, he urged me on to continue. I was surprised by how nice he was, that he would notice other people around him. We began speaking but I don't really remember who initiated the conversation. In all honesty it was probably him who spoke first. It fell silent for a minute. We were sitting on the bench at the local school gym. I just turned my attention to my basketball and baseball cards. As I began shuffling through them he noticed and he said, "Dude can I have that one?! - I'll trade with you." I was caught off guard. I didn't even know which one he was talking about and so I just looked at him and said nothing. I imagine my look insinuated the question to him, "Which one?" or "Watchu got?" I then asked him. He went to his backpack immediately and pulled out a ton of baseball cards, basketball cards, and football cards.

"Which one do you want?" he urged me on.

"Which one do you want?" I said right back to him.

"That Scottie Pippen card. Which one do you want?" he asked me again.

"Well do you have a John Starks card, I haven't found one at the pawn shop here?" I replied to Blake.

"Yeah," he replied as he eagerly searched in his bag to get it to me. "Oh man, I have that at home but we can go over there if that's cool," Blake said invitingly.

We headed over to his house after practice that day. I don't even remember which other cards I gathered for him to trade with each other. Truth be told it didn't matter to me. This kid loved basketball and so did I. We knew that we were friends immediately. "I'm Dan," I let him know. "Yeah I know, I'm Blake," he told me. We traded and fist bumped as if we went back a long time ago. We clicked up from that moment on throughout the rest of my elementary schooling. We did everything together. Both of us thought that we would be NBA players one day. We were best friends. I later found out that he was Mormon, but I made no distinction between his religion nor mine, we were kindred spirits. We enjoyed riding bikes together and hanging out. We did share our religious stories and he was as knowledgeable about his faith as I was about mine. The first time that I went over to Blake's house I couldn't believe how big it was. His pantry and refrigerator was always full. Looking back on this, I wondered if they were low-key survivalists. I always felt like a little explorer running through there. He had four siblings and he was the youngest. We were nice to one another but we didn't really hangout. Blake and I were almost inseparable.

One thing that Blake and I had in common was our taste in music. We listened to music that ranged from Coolio's Gangster's Paradise to Whoomp There It Is!, by Tag Team. Even though the nineties was a decade replete of one hit wonders. We listened to Mambo No. 5 once, however Blake wasn't even aware of some of the riskier songs that were popular in those days. Maybe it was due to the fact he was Mormon. One of those songs is by Shaggy, It Wasn't Me. It was always hilarious to catch other kids singing that song. That conversation would typically begin when another kid would be singing the song in the lunch-line or in the library. Just breaking it down, this is how the conversation would start, "I even had her in the shower, WASN'T ME…She even caught me on camera, WASN'T ME!", the anonymous person would sing melodically. "Oh, you know that song too?!", I would ask, as if I was surprised after the thirtieth time. "Yeah, duh.", anonymous kid would answer. My generation also popularized the famous "yo mama" jokes. I threw that joke at many kids. Blake and I just got along great. We would watch and re-watch Space Jam featuring Michael Jordan. The Lion King ushered in a new era for Disney, and Toy Story also placed Pixar films on the map. These movies and songs fed into my general happy disposition.

One instance that comes to mind about this period in my life is when we had Blake over at my grandparents' house to play pool. My grandparents liked this kid, even though my grandfather resented the fact that he was Mormon. I think that I may have enjoyed the nineties most when I was with, either my grandparents, or when I was hanging out with Blake. When we hung out at my grandparents we would eat outdated snacks from the pantry. My grandparents had snacks but they never snacked on stuff, so they would be stale. Blake and I spent hours outside shooting hoops. If we were tired of being outside we would play dominoes with my grandma. At other times, when the weather wasn't ideal for playing sports outside, we spent some time inside playing pool with my grandpa. It was a joyful time for me.

Another great thing about this friend was that I never felt on guard with him. I did enjoy speaking to his siblings and parents often and we always had fun activities lined up to do, but I never felt on guard. We would hang and it was perfect. His house was so big that there wasn't a shortage of things to do. We would kill ants outside with pesticides, we jumped on the trampoline, we played basketball or soccer, and we also built things with Legos. If we got hungry we would make nachos. One day Blake and I were hanging out in the woods downhill from his house and we decided that it would be a good idea to trek back to his home to have something to drink. On our way back Blake broke the silence and just asked me, "What happened to your dad?" - dead silence. I even stopped walking. I was thinking to myself, "Ugh, there's that question again." I couldn't tell him that I didn't have one. "Of course everyone has a dad, so I have to come up with something here," that was the idea crossed through my mind. I would wonder where my dad was at, but I didn't miss him per se because I didn't know him. I missed the idea of him. "My mom is dating an undercover agent," I replied almost robotically. He thought that it was cool. I coupled the story with my love for geography and history. I made the story credible enough for him to believe. The walk was a bit awkward after that for me but I was relieved to see his house at the top of the hill. We walked around towards the front of the house and made our way up the steep driveway. Once we reached the top I was happy to draw nearer to the front door. He never brought the question up again.

Some more time had passed and we were in the middle of fall in the fifth grade. I finished up the year and I was eager to hit the summer with my bud Blake. Before the summertime hit, my mom was having trouble with Tammy. Mom had kept a friendship with Angelina throughout this entire time, however they were never romantic again. Mom and Tammy eventually broke up and I was glad to hear the news. Tammy was jealous that my mother had this friendship and maybe this was a catalyst for them to leave each other. This was good news to me because, then I wouldn't have to lie about my mom's relationship, she was no longer in one. I could just say she was single and I could speak the truth for once. I went on to enjoy the better part of the summer with Blake. As the summer was drawing to an end I was eager to begin a new school year as a middle schooler. Suddenly, one day I overheard my grandparents speaking as I was visiting them. They were talking about me moving away. "Where to?", I thought to myself. I didn't speak to them about it but I waited to hear from my mom to see what she would tell me. I was hoping so much that a day wouldn't come where she would tell me that this was true. I would miss my friend so much. I would miss my grandparents. A couple of days later she sat me down in our living room, just the both of us, she told me that we would be moving to Phoenix. "Why?", I thought to myself. I loved visiting Phoenix but I didn't know anyone there. I didn't have my school there nor did I have any friends there. "What about grandma and grandpa?" I asked almost pleadingly. I didn't understand. She let me know that she had a friend there and we were moving there so that mom could be closer to her. I already knew what that was about. I knew that I had to leave my friend, my grandparents, my church, my school, and my familiar world to this future that I definitely wasn't sure about. Turns out my mom had seen a newspaper ad of a person who was scouting for a partner with similar interests. She lived in Phoenix and that was reason enough to uproot our lives in Pinetop-Lakeside to move there. I was being stripped of everything that I loved. The things that I cherished would soon be gone.

From the moment that my mom told my grandparents of her plans to move away, they worried for me. They didn't want us to move but my mother was set on making this transition. I broke the news to Blake and I remember hanging out with his family and I thought the world would end for him as I thought that it was ending for me. My childhood expectations were gone. It was difficult for him but life would move on for him and I didn't think that it would move on for me at all. The most difficult thing for me was saying good-bye to my grandparents. Before the end of the summer we packed my mother's pickup truck with of our things. We were hanging out at my grandparents' house at first. My mom had something quick to do at the post office before we left and it would be there that we would say good-bye to each other. On the way there I was trying to take it all in. The wind struck my face and it felt sweeter than ever but I also felt a ball well up inside my stomach. Once they were in sight I was excited and sad all at once. I hopped out and ran to them. I embraced them long and hard. I thought that maybe I would never see them again, I thought that I wouldn't visit Pinetop ever again. I had never seen my grandfather cry until this day. This just settled the uncertainty for me even more. I think that they were unsure and sad for me as well. They exchanged some words very softly, but I couldn't hear them, almost as if my sense of sight was engaged more in the hopes of not missing a thing. I was trying to sear their face into my brain. I was trying to make memories that could last me forever. Their smell was so sweet as I gave them that hug that day, however the feeling was somber. Then just like that, we left for Phoenix.

CHAPTER 3
JEZEBEL, QUEEN OF HATE

When we arrived to Phoenix, it was quiet in the truck. All of the Senita and Saguaro cacti were passing us by. I remember thinking that I would be there forever. I wished that we would never arrive, better yet, I wished that we would just go back to Pinetop-Lakeside. I had never met her new partner, so it was bound to be awkward. We were going to move into a stranger's apartment, it was a bizarre feeling to say the least. We pulled up to her home in Chandler, Arizona, an incorporated town to the greater Phoenix area. We pulled up to the gated community and my mom called her. This was when mom had one of the LG flip-phones. Her lady friend let us in and gave us directions to the apartment. She and my mother embraced and then she quickly introduced herself to me saying, "Hi I am Joo-aaan Goldstein, with only one 'n' at the end of Joan." She extended her hand to me. I reluctantly responded, "I am Dan", as I reached for hers. I now think the way she introduced herself to me makes a lot of sense, given her personality that I experienced throughout my mother's six year relationship with her. In any case, it is spelled Joan so she should have just pronounced it like that. It just seemed like too much effort on her part. She had a firm grip and very big hands in comparison to mine. We didn't have much with us so we began to unpack our things and began to settle our belongings inside. I will say that "Joan" is the main reason that I am using alternate names in this book because, she would without question sue me for 'detraction' to her character. I also decided to give her a Jewish last name because she had an open disdain for Jewish people, some poetic justice of my own. You will found out momentarily why.

Once I stepped into the apartment the inside confirmed that it was a one bedroom, one bathroom apartment. I realized that my mother was settling her things in Joan's room, so I wondered where I would be sleeping. Mom didn't bother to let me know that I wouldn't have a room. I was only a kid so I wasn't too sure what was going on, but the terrible planning and lack of communication that occurred in this situation would reap some heartache for years to come. My mom felt guilty during this time, but not guilty enough to make sure that I was looked out for properly. I didn't have a room and I felt that mom didn't care for me. I felt that I didn't fit in with my own mom at all. They then showed me a small green Coleman inflatable mattress waiting for me in the living room. It was next to her sheep dog, Rufus. He was pretty mellow. She absolutely adored him. He just looked at mom and I, but he wasn't curious enough to get up and greet us. I'll blame it on his age. It wasn't terribly late into the day so I was wondering if we would be eating next. "Let me give you guys a tour of the apartment complex then we'll come back here and get ready to grab a bite," Joan said, almost as if she read my mind. I went outside, maybe a bit hopeful that I would like my stay here. Man was I wrong.

It was a hot summer day and the sun shone bright as the warmth hit my face. I just wanted to be home and that was it. She led us outside, and we simply followed. She took us around and showed us the basketball courts and it had two swimming pools as well. I would have loved to take a dip right then but it wasn't the time. Then right after she showed us the gym, where a couple of residents were making good use of the equipment. I remember thinking that this was all cool. I thought that I might like it because of the atmosphere, and it had decent amenities, so I would give this place a chance. We made it back to the apartment eventually and then we washed up to dine-out that night. It was probably a fancy restaurant, I cannot remember the name of the place for the life of me. Joan was accustomed to the finer things in life. The 'nicer' things in life never compensate for what truly matters. It is something that I have to constantly remind myself of today.

Come to think of it, my mom had bought me nice clothes and toys to keep me happy, as if these things could bring me fulfillment. Kids at school liked hanging out with me partly because of my facade, but I was also always dressed to impress, and this made me cool. I made them believe that I had a great home life but none of them knew what I had to go home to. My mom was uninvolved in my life, and the gifts were supposed to fill that gap. No way! Kids do not want to have nice things above meaningful relationships, because at the end of the day they are just things and they cannot have a lasting effect on them. They want you to be a parent. Your kids want you because that is what will help form them for their lives ahead of them. No, I didn't have a dad but that doesn't mean that I had to lose my mom also. That is what it felt like. Mom had given Joan precedence over me, and the damage was near irreparable.

Joan had, and may still have a reputation for leaving a lot of damage and pain in her wake. A little bit of history on Joan, she is from Medford, Oregon. Both of her parents were from California and her mother used to be a model in the Medford area as a young woman. Joan was tall, slender, and athletic looking. She played volleyball in high school and was popular for it. She had a brief relationship with another girl who played volleyball while she was in school. Her skills were good enough to get her into college to play, but she didn't quite make the cut beyond that. She didn't graduate from college. I don't know, maybe this was one of the underlying causes for her discontentment in life. She married after a few years during her studies in Oregon. Her first husband was her high school sweetheart. Their marriage lasted a few years. Based upon what Joan shared with my mother, their marriage ended in a rupture rather than being one that fizzled out. She was married to this man for ten years and then she eventually handed him some divorce papers. The circumstances leading up to the divorce are pretty revealing of her character. He used to own a logging company in Oregon. One day, accidentally, a truck full of logs and lumber shifted. The timber fell onto him. He was severely injured and he lost mobility in his legs. He was unable to manage the business so Joan had to step in to take over. Several issues ensued following the ill-fated accident. Aside from the obvious fact that they couldn't have sex, the business eventually went belly up due to mismanagement. As a couple, they incurred much debt from the medical procedures to improve her husband's condition. The procedures were to no avail. Joan let it slip once to my mother that she had continued her superfluous spending during the whole time after the surgeries. She couldn't be with him, and she 'let him know' that it was all his fault that he was injured. She left him, she left her high school sweetheart. What a shame, not for him, but for her. Her lack of integrity would explain why the room would drop a couple of degrees in temperature when she would step in. Mom and I hadn't the slightest clue what a shit storm we were really in.

She met her next husband in Oregon as well. This story is just as revealing of her character as the first. Her second husband was a lawyer. He was apparently well off. This second marriage lasted five years, maybe longer. Turns out he was gay. Joan maybe had some clues about this before she married him, not that he acted on his attraction for men or anything of the sort, but she nonetheless decided to marry him. They eventually divorced. She was able to attain some of his assets and thus was able to pay for a house later on. My mother and I factor into this a bit later on, but after we lived in her apartment for some time.

Eventually Joan got a job at the Scottsdale, Arizona Fashion Square Mall. She worked at a store called Harry and David. They sell many products from Oregon. Among these were jars of jam, pears, and boxed chocolates fit for a Valentine's Day present, if things are serious. She enjoyed fine dining and would frequently buy her groceries from expensive grocery stores. We were simpler people, small town folk you can say, especially in comparison to Joan and her lifestyle. I think this could have been one factor that intrigued my mom to stay with her in the first place. Admittedly so, it was interesting for me to expand my knowledge of food and music during this time, one of the very few positives during this period in my life. She took a lot of pride in her appearance. I still distinctively remember the smell of her Ralph Lauren Blue perfume. She dressed nicely and she wouldn't shop for her clothes at places aside from the mall where she worked. She also loved to drink Foster's Australian beer, Paulaner Hefeweizen, and liquor on the weekends. She probably drank alcohol four days out of the week. I think maybe she was coping because of the several setbacks she had in her life.

One example of this is when she relocated to Chandler, Arizona to join a golf academy. Evidently she stopped pursuing that when she realized that, just like her volleyball days, this would go nowhere for her either. If she hadn't moved to Arizona, would we have met…? Once again, it no use to mull over hypotheticals. Her mother passed from cancer not to long before she moved to Arizona, and she told my mother that she was the one person that helped ground her. It was a long arduous process for her. People handle adversity differently, and some handle it better than others do. My take on it is that everybody's got heartache to deal with, so we do eventually have to face it.

That was her story up until she met us. We returned to the apartment that night however, and my mom and Joan retired to their bedroom. I remember sleeping on that green inflatable mattress thinking to myself, "Fuck, my mom is gay, and she is living with a woman!" That was a strong thought coming from me because I was taught by my grandparents, not only to refrain from cussing, but to also avoid thinking them. I figured that I could block that out of my mind and just focus on school that would be coming up in less than two weeks.

Before those two weeks were up I felt awkward around my mother and her new girlfriend. I had plenty of time to be by myself and kids' minds wander just as much as adults do. I constantly wished to be somewhere else, almost anywhere else rather than there with Joan. I was always walking on eggshells, but I think I would have preferred to walk on burning coals and embers, if it meant that I could just zip away from there, even momentarily. My grandparents were seemingly gone from my life, my mom had given preference to Joan over me, and I was no longer involved in the church or hanging out with my friends on a regular basis. All of the positive people and outlets were stripped from my life. Yes, I would have preferred to walk on those coals and embers. School was just around the corner, and that was potentially a plus to look forward to.

I enrolled in the middle school as a sixth grader. I was nervous to begin this stage. I didn't know anyone. It was definitely intimidating. The school was a little ghetto. My mother told me one day as we were reflecting on our story that she didn't like the atmosphere at my school there. The school was overpopulated and she thinks that we were treated like cattle, administrators and teachers herding us along from one place to another. On my first day there, there was a fight between a black dude and a Mexican dude. It was over a girl named Paprika, this sums up what sort of school this was. My schooling at this point began to be interrupted. We moved around a ton. A word of advice, if for a legitimate reason parents find themselves having to move frequently, please ensure that your children's education remains consistent. This is extremely important. That means, be involved. Mom had little involvement in my schooling, and I struggled. I particularly didn't like mathematics or science. I did always have an affinity for geography and history, and I was okay at English, but I struggled with the rest. If my academic proficiency were to be correlated on a graph this would be the beginning of a downwards slope in most subjects but that fact became more evident as time progressed. I still didn't lose my touch with people and I was able to make friends quickly. They weren't tremendous connections though because I was new. Unfortunately this was short lived because unsuspectingly, I had to move to a neighboring school soon. I only stayed there one semester of the sixth grade. My mom wanted me to be in a better school and in a better area. Once again, all I needed was a caring home and maybe mom wasn't fit to provide that for me. She was constantly working and she had to commute forty-five minutes to work every weekday so she needed someone to take care of me. Joan was less than willing to do so.

I moved in with my aunt Mary and uncle Buck in the West Valley, the greater Phoenix area is simply known as the West Valley. They were nice people and my aunt was a bit loud and talkative. Uncle Buck was quiet, nice, and smart. He seemed a more mellow version of my grandfather. They had a beautiful home complete with a pool and a fenced in yard. They had televisions and computers. It was elegantly furnished. I almost couldn't believe it, to hear from them that I would have my own room was consoling. My oldest cousin from their family was out of high school. She worked. My other cousin is a male, and he is a year younger than me. We played often. He also had a brother that was older than me, he attended the same high school. My aunt and uncle were generous with me. They were always pleasant people but I never felt at home with them. I always lacked my mother's affection during that semester. The crazy thing was that even though I had people around me I felt like a loner, and I was a loner. I would retreat into my room often and think to myself. I just had to learn to be by myself. They didn't know but I would lie down on the floor and cry by myself at times and I longed for some companionship. Their cordiality couldn't replace the gaping hole that could only be filled by my mom. My religious background forced me to turn to God and ask him why I was in this situation. Silence. Was this unspeakable too? Could I not receive an answer to this as well? Did I not deserve a response? Could he not give me a reason why my mom was so distant from me, or why she had chosen Joan over me? Only with time would I begin to discover some answers to my many questions. I learned to be with that silence a bit, because my mother would also offer me the same silence because we were distant. I moved back in with her and Joan and I thought that this may help remedy some of that distance, but I was in for a rude awakening.

I remember a distinctive thought that I had while still in the sixth grade, that I wanted to be wherever God wasn't. I wanted to hide from him like Adam had tried in Eden, the difference was that in my eyes I had done nothing wrong. In fact I did everything right, I was generally well-behaved, I applied myself in school, and I prayed. I bent my knees to him and he saw me cry, he saw my lips move but I didn't think that he was deaf. Adam was unsuccessful at hiding from him and so was I. I didn't blame God for 'causing' this isolation in my life but he didn't intervene when I thought that I needed him the most. I think that he granted me my sincerest request to let me hide from him a little, God's own hand at poetic justice. I felt this more undoubtedly when I moved back in with my mom and Joan. Joan had used some of her divorce settlement assets to buy a house south of Phoenix in San Tan Valley, Arizona. She eventually had her grandmother move from a convalescent home in with us. We called her Mimi. She was such a sweet lady. I was glad to know that I would still have a room to call my own so I didn't mind an extra body in the house at all. Maybe this room was a refuge from Joan, my mom, from God even.

That refuge was easily laid to waste whenever Joan was around. She wasn't fair at all to us nor to her own grandmother. Her grandmother was living with us and Joan collected her monthly income. My mom and I now suspect that she most likely moved her grandmother in because, aside from the money she collected from her, she was expecting an inheritance once Mimi would pass away. Love clearly wasn't Joan's motivation for moving her into the apartment. My mom and I now can easily say that she was just using her grandma. Joan yelled at her constantly, I mean how do you yell at your own grandmother? She made her cry and she belittled her. How could she do that? I couldn't believe how so much hate could exist in a person. As more time passed, and I experienced more harshness from her, it began to make sense how hate could spring up in our hearts. Maybe something happened in her life that made her act this way towards others. It still isn't an excuse to treat each other like that.

A prime example of how Joan could spew so much venom to me was by blatantly showing her distaste for me. One instance was after her sheep dog died. She mourned her loss. Once she had warmed up to the idea of her old dog being gone she decided she would have to get another pet. She eventually ended up getting a basset hound from a pet store in the mall. She paid over several hundred dollars for the puppy.

A few weeks after her purchase I was loading the dishwasher one day and I didn't hear the dog had followed my trail. It, out of curiosity, had approached me from behind. I took a step backwards as I was finishing up and I sort of stepped on the dogs paw and I heard it yelp. I jerked my leg up as my body was half twisting to see what had happened. I was simultaneously trying to get out of there, maybe I could on time. I lost my balance and tumbled backwards and I banged the back of my head on the doorknob. BANG! The impact slammed the door shut. Then I thudded to the ground. The sound reverberated throughout the entire house, but then it was still and quiet for a moment. No blood I hoped. I clutched my throbbing head in my hands and curled up my body as Joan turned the corner into the kitchen. She saw the puppy had scampered away from me and noticed that I was holding my head. "You're so stupid you know!" she sneered at me through gritted teeth as her nose twitched. She yelled at me and said that the dog was worth more than I was. I paused there in pain as my mother quickly followed behind her. She heard the whole ordeal. She said nothing to Joan but she asked me if I was okay. "I hit my head mom! No, I am not okay." I ran to my room to retreat. "I am not worthless", I thought to myself in that quiet bedroom. My mom's fear, timidity, and outright refusal to stand up for me was pretty characteristic of her during that terrible relationship. I was mad at Joan but I was more angry at my mother for saying nothing. Mom didn't stick up for me at all, and this happened all the time. I was attempting to retreat but I just stewed over this in my head and in my heart. I didn't hate her but I definitely resented the fact that she didn't take a stand for me. I think because of this I really have trouble with phlegmatic people. It is very difficult for me to tolerate people who straddle fences and wait for the dust to settle before making decisions. I can't stand the non-committal attitude. This was just the beginning of Joan's abuse towards me, but then her abuse began to slowly pervade the entire household.

The welcome wasn't warm from Joan to begin with. My distaste for her grew. It was infectious. No one was off limits at Joan's house. I used to have to clean up after Mimi all of the time because Joan refused to do it, and she would be out with my mom having fun while I was stuck at the house. This wasn't home for me at all. Up until this point I hadn't had a true home the way I conceived of it, but this without a doubt wasn't supposed to be it. At one point Mom and Joan decided that they'd like to take a trip to Las Vegas, and they left Mimi and I alone at the house for the weekend. She had dementia but she was present enough to do some things on her own. I remember having to make her breakfast and a fresh pot of coffee every morning. It was probably a master gourmet meal in my mind, but she was fed so it was more than passable. That weekend was the first among many in which Mimi would soil the toilet seat without noticing it. I had to clean up the mess. I guess my mom and Joan thought that from this moment on I would be Mimi's personal pooper-scooper. Increasingly I grew very bitter at Joan and towards my mother even. Somehow I could pick out the difference between their attitude and Mimi's. Mimi didn't have a say at all in this matter. That was something that Mimi and I shared in common. Mom had a say here but she didn't voice an opinion. I could never tell if she had an opinion about this type of treatment towards me or Mimi, but if she did, it didn't matter enough for her to voice it. I began to wonder if she ever would take a stand. Luckily, I didn't hold my breath.

The second time that mom and Joan left Mimi and I in San Tan Valley, they both took a trip to Palm Springs, California to visit Joan's dad. As a child I couldn't think of a good enough reason for anyone to leave their kid to take yet another weekend trip with someone as abusive and vile as Joan. Another time they went to Oregon to visit Joan's family and friends. I felt that mom didn't give 'f' about me. This was truly a puzzling question to me for the longest time. Unanswered questions of this nature stand in innumerable children's minds as to why a parent would do that to them. It was the worst year of my life.

I don't want to demonize Joan at all, but there is clearly a strong case against her attitude towards everyone. I was still ashamed of my mother's orientation, so after a while I suppressed those thoughts. I pushed them to the back of my mind. Mom's sexuality didn't percolate in the forefront of my mind all of the time. I wasn't the only person to receive verbal abuse from Joan because eventually my mother began to as well, and my mother would just take it and not say a word. Silence from her lips. Silence from me also. Silence from Mimi. Silence from God. Who could I tell? The silence indicated to me that there was no one who did care. Would I tell my mother that I felt scared at times. No, I didn't feel like this would have moved her to stand up for me or for Mimi. Could I tell my grandparents that Joan's words were only words but it felt like violence against my person, it felt like violence against me? No. In fact I already had told them. I called them one day hoping that they could help me escape from that mess. They never realized that it was that bad. They couldn't have imagined that my mother had allowed us to continue in such an abusive situation. They told me to just trust my mother. Sometimes the only thing that can be done when one is in between a rock and hard place is to just take the beating. I was already beginning to not trust my mom because I sincerely felt that I couldn't go to her for anything. I just took the beating. I had begun to count God out. I didn't really consider Mimi an alternative though we spoke maybe as far as the normal formalities would go, but she and I had more in common than I could have realized. We were both unwanted by Joan it seemed, and my mother wouldn't fend for us. I just couldn't get it. Mom didn't even fend for herself. I later on asked her why it was that she allowed all of this to happen to us. She was very dependent on Joan. It also seems that Joan needed someone that was just as insecure as she was, to lean on as a crutch. Mom needed someone to please in order to feel validated, and Joan needed someone to impose her will on, it was the perfect storm. Joan was scared to be alone, but she was emotionally ill-equipped to love anyone aside from her own-self. I can now see a bit more clearly where my mother was coming from. Didn't I want the same validation that she desired? We lacked communication and this was one of the biggest killers in our relationship. As a kid, I couldn't place my finger on it. Time doesn't heal all wounds, it can some, but this required effort.

Mom and I talk about these things now and we would even revisit some of these difficult times as adults, in an attempt to understand one another. At one point during my time in seminary we were hashing all of these things out and she let me know, "I catered to her because I felt that if I pleased her, then her temper would ease up a bit. I figured that if she could have a good day then we could have a good day. If she just accepted us then we would be fine." When talking about this, I remember relating to her. I was pretty much in the same mode, I felt the need to be accepted, so I did what I thought was necessary. This need for validation also skulked into my adolescence and even my adulthood. I answered her with a sigh, "That sounds exhausting, to fight for someone's approval so much that you aren't yourself anymore." I paused momentarily and then I continued. "Maybe we have more in common than I have suspected." She agreed. A little understanding goes a long way.

That year in seventh grade was difficult, that's an understatement. Joan began taking a turn for the worst. She and my mom would drink several times during the week. Joan drank beer almost daily. She would yell at me for the smallest of reasons. It almost seemed like she was looking for something, anything to be angry at. I was sad a lot of the time. At school I couldn't let this be shown. Causing laughter was an extremely important strategy in my arsenal. It became second nature for me to be the funny guy in school. This provided an easy avenue to make good conversation with girls, maybe swoon a couple of them in history class, as early as the seventh grade. I think that it helped since I was in my element. I thrived in history class, and geography was a piece of cake. I even became a sort of star pupil and kind of a teacher's pet. He thought that I was in the gifted program and he even mentioned it to me once. I didn't stop him, he believed what I wanted him to believe, and that was fine with me. It is like that kid who wants street credit because he lets everyone think that he is from the ghetto when in reality he is from the suburbs. Simultaneously, midway through junior high it was becoming apparent that I struggled much with most things mathematic, and with science. Needless to say when my teacher, Mr.

Fletcher found out about how I was marginally close to failing math, he was shocked. He pull me aside when our dismissal bell rang. "Dan, are you failing math?", he questioned as the kids were funneling into the hallway. "Uh... no, but I could use some help." "Well you know I can help you whenever you need it right? Yeah, just swing by whenever, alright?", he offered. "Okay," I agreed. I never went to him for help but I squeaked by in math that year. Lying by omitting the truth and telling a lie. I could do it all. This was the only other skill that rivaled my history and geography skills. I lied to become who I thought I should be but the sad truth is that I wasn't really showing what I was really experiencing, definitely not at school because I was hurting deeply inside. I needed validation, I needed to be accepted for who I truly was but I thought that this shouldn't include my depressiveness and despair brought from home. This hurt was not me, but it was a part of me, and I couldn't make that distinction.

I am not saying that I was a complete hypocrite because there are more layers to a person than there are shades between black and white. There are more layers to a person than just their emotions, though they should be considered. The neglect that I received from my mom during this entire time, and the abusive language that Joan would spit at me caused a great disparity between who I was becoming and who I pretended to be. There was always an issue with Joan. I believed that God existed but I began to doubt his goodness. I began to also lose faith in people.

I could only come to understand this contrast with some reflection on it, presently, as a man. Much of the reflection that I've done, I would do while traveling abroad. Maybe this helped me step out of myself a little and consider myself more deeply. I realized that I have always had a sense of humor, but I really upped this part of my life at school so that all of the jocks and class clowns would accept me. This reminds me of Emilio Estevez's character in the Breakfast Club. I know that this movie was released in the mid-eighties, but it perfectly describes my generation. I was like Andrew Clark, I always had to achieve something for someone else rather than understanding and accepting that it was okay to just be myself. This caused me to be who I really wasn't so that I could be validated. I didn't think that it was okay to show my true emotions. It wouldn't have mattered to express them at home anyway, who would listen? I always passed it off as if things were cool at home. I have always had a poker face. I am a master at masking sadness. This is when I learned to smile a lot even though I felt terrible inside. So an analogy then, I felt that my only option was to play the card that would win the game, even if it meant hiding cards up my sleeve.

As to my relationship with God, I stopped trusting him. I asked myself and I would ask him why he would want me in such a situation. I didn't get an answer from him. I yearned for good friends but I couldn't let them get close beyond a certain point, given the circumstances. My friends would have me over for sleep overs, but I wouldn't return the favor. Let me clarify, I couldn't return the favor. I couldn't ever let anybody know certain things about my life. It would have proved too fatal to my facade. It would be in shambles and how could I be cool after that? This caused a problem because one of my buddies' mother asked why the boys couldn't stay over at my house this once. "Ahhh… this weekend isn't good because we have a ton of people over, sorry dude," I countered. I was a good defensive conversationalist without seeming defensive at all. I wanted to tell the truth and do what was right, but God put me in this situation and he was the only one to blame in my eyes. It was a big contrast though, between my persona at school and what I was really feeling. It was a dark time. I prayed to God that he would just take my life away. Despair is a scary thing. This pushed me to have suicidal thoughts. I didn't have the means to carry this out, but if I had maybe there wouldn't much of a story to read at all today. Who knows what shape my mother would have been in if I had taken my life. While on my computer one day, I even searched for ways to kill myself. I saw that swallowing pills was an option, but I didn't have any on hand. I didn't have a pistol either, but if I had… who knows. I did attempt it once and luckily my tools and knowledge needed to execute my plan were very limited.

One day I came home from school. It was a normal day by all appearances. However, appearances can be very deceiving. Each human being is a world unto himself. No one person views or handles reality and life the exact same as another, but I was so terribly without hope for my life at home that I seriously considered ending everything. Once I stepped into the house I saw my mom in the living room. The hairs on the back of my neck were standing up and I had a heightened sense of things. Time seemed to slow down at first, and there was just the moment. I remember feeling that time had ceased to exist and I was trying to take my mom's face and sear it into my mind. "This is the last time that I am going to see you mom," I thought to myself with a heart filled with sadness. I said hi to mom. I then grabbed a couple of her boxcutters with the intention of opening up my veins. I went to my room and I thought to myself, "This is it. I will be gone and it will be nothing for mom. She won't miss me at all because I was exactly that in her life, nothing." It had to be done, I didn't matter and I was tired of not mattering to anyone.

I made sure the door was locked. I laid the blades on my bed and I grabbed one. I cut my wrist from one side to the other. I had pressed the blade pretty hard into my wrist but I wasn't cut that deeply. I remember it hurting and stinging like a bitch and it only served to frustrate me further. I threw the blade across my room then I cried bitterly from anger and frustration. I didn't have the know how nor the resources to be done with this world, but I felt very convinced that THAT was what I wanted! Some people say that suicide is an act of cowardice, and it certainly goes against my faith, but it seems like a step that requires a degree of bravery to execute. Committing suicide is a decisive move. If I had a gun in the house as a lonely thirteen year old, I probably would have taken my life. Death is scary, but life can be equally as scary it seems. At times it is difficult to live well. Life still must be chosen, life must still be lived. Let me just add that if a relationship of yours, or a lack of a relationship pushes you to think about committing suicide, don't. If you think suicide is the answer, please don't take that route. Just think about it, when you make it through, you could write a book about it. I have enjoyed life, laughter, and healing much since I was a child. There is opportunity to grow, we just have to find those opportunities.

After my failed attempt, I searched for meaning in my life. We are supposed have parents who willingly teach us these valuable lessons. I didn't have the perfect parents to help guide me, but then again who has perfect parents to guide them? There is always a certain amount of stumbling and searching that we will have to do on our own, in order to find meaning in life. I began stumbling, and yes I began my search.

In my search I had to examine myself deeply. It hurt, but I had to also examine this extremely low point in my life. I attempted to commit suicide, and it speaks to the fact that it is important to be aware of the state of our children. Furthermore, it speaks how much we really need each other. It speaks of how much true communication is needed. I speak of our society as a whole. I didn't think or reflect on growth but I did want good things in life. I wanted my mother to notice me, I wanted a family life. I began to search for validation but as far the family part, I wasn't going to find it at home so it had to be found elsewhere. Most of all I wanted to be away from Joan. Even though my relationship with God was on the decline I still asked him to take Joan away from us, to take Joan from me. I think that we are like that often times when dealing with faith. We sincerely ask for things and this is good, but sometimes we cannot even begin to imagine the possible implications of our wishes. My mother's relationship with Joan was beginning to get rockier than usual. Joan worsened things because she would drink more often than usual and a bit of a rift was created between the both of them. This caused my mother and I to eventually move to Ahwatukee in South Phoenix. They needed some time and distance apparently to make things work, but some things are unworkable.

We moved fifty minutes northeast of Joan who was down in San Tan Valley and Queen Creek area. Finally, a sigh of relief. We do that often don't we? We focus so much on our problems at hand and are so consumed by them that we often miss the bigger picture of life. I was very happy at first because Joan was not in the picture. My mother would visit her some but she fell into a huge rut. We moved into a two bedroom and two bathroom apartment at Portofino apartments. I didn't notice my mother at first, I was just relieved to have my mom to myself, though she was not handling the breakup very well. I wasn't that aware of my mom's thought on the separation but I was happy. I am not being retaliatory, but it is necessary to be honest with ourselves. In this spirit, here is something I would like to say directly to Joan.

Dear Joan,

If you ever read this I know your first reaction will be uncontrollable anger. Then you will explore options on how to sue me for defaming your "good name." Then you will get drunk on Foster's beer and rant to anyone who may be around you that you're not this kind of person and you will speak of all the good things you did for us. Then you will get even more drunk and start listening to Celine Dion and eventually convince yourself that you are a good person. Let's be honest, we know that's not true. My mom believes there is hope for you. However, I'm more of a realist, and I believe that you will always be self-absorbed and alone. I still have not found it in me to fully forgive you because you were always so abusive. I don't ever wish anything bad upon you and I sincerely wish you the best, but so far I can't forgive you. I hope someday I can. You mentally abused us and preyed on the vulnerable, and you Joan, will have to answer to God for this. I know that you will probably die alone with no loved ones around, and no one to care about you, except for maybe a dog that you just bought a few months before the fact. So when you are on your death bed, my advice is to turn to God because he is the only one rooting for you. Good luck.

When we first moved out my happiness radar was beeping. As I entered the seventh grade I was starting yet another new school. Akimel Middle School. I noticed all of the cool kids, and I could easily fit in. How do I break the ice here? Where should I say I was from? I was once asked if I was from Hawaii so I decided to go with that. I employed like a rhetorical jiu-jitsu. Whatever came my way, if it didn't fit the persona that I was creating for myself, then I would find a way to twist it to my advantage. I described the 'ocean' in great detail. I used to go 'surfing' some mornings before school. I understood Hawaiian culture and I always had an answer if asked about it. I was still well versed in history and biographies and I loved watching documentaries on National Geographic and the History Channel, so my skills stayed polished. These were the good ol' days when there were documentaries on significant historical events and people, and the focus wasn't on the guy with the wild hair who was obsessed with aliens and supposed UFO sightings. I would learn from the show because it interested me, but evidently I wasn't as interested in other subjects. My teachers began to take notice that my math skills were not on par with my history and writings skills, but they helped provide me with tutoring services. In all honesty some of them were a little too generous with me. My prowess at the lying game was hard to rival. If I couldn't be accepted for who I was then I would find a way to have people accept me. This brought me some level of happiness and contentment at school. At home with mom though, I realized that there was this painful monotony that was rarely broken. I would do some of my homework after school, but I would typically hang out with my friends rather than focusing on school. We did a lot of walking around town. Our usual spot to hang out was the Taco Bell. We would talk about girls and which one of them we thought was the cutest. Yes, for the most part I was content during this time but I would rarely see my mother, and what could substitute her in my life? Often times in life there are trade-offs. Yeah the grass is greener on the other side of the fence, but this grass can wither more just as easily and sometimes it does when we don't expect it. No matter how much I could try to have friends, which I was undoubtedly successful at, I couldn't get beyond the fact that mom wasn't really around.

Mom was constantly working. I would come home from school or sometimes I would be out with my buddies hanging all afternoon, and it would soon be time for me to start getting ready for bed. Sometimes I would be fast asleep, sometimes I was still up in my room, mom would get in from her long day at work and I just knew that I wouldn't be seeing her. I wouldn't see her unless it was on the weekends. Even then it was not a real guarantee. It's crazy to know how she still affected my life without really being there. Co-dependency can cripple our relationships. My mom is a prime example of how this can happen. My mom would commute to see her and that sometimes meant an entire weekend, which we were supposed to spend together, was gone. She was in a deep funk. She just couldn't help being away from Joan. As I asked her why did they break up, mom answered, "It was really because Joan was a super bitch. At one point we were arguing on the phone and she called me a CUNT. That was it for me, and I told her that we were over, then I hung up." I know you are thinking what I am thinking, thaaat's why she broke up with her? WTF? Yeah, there is something incongruous about that, it's just off. Their entire relationship was as off balanced and this was the tipping point. The final straw doesn't seem significant until it breaks the camel's back.

Well… I was glad that mom and I could at least agree that Joan had to go. "You know Dan I think that things would have been a lot better if she wasn't in the picture," mom tells me. "Yeah, no shit," I thought, but I didn't say it to her. Obviously I'm of the same opinion. I questioned her, "Why would you still see her?" I suppose I was just escaping," was her answer. "Escaping from what mom?", I asked. "I was in bad way financially, I wasn't really stable. I needed to be away from that, but it wasn't that I really missed Joan as much as I was keeping up the co-dependency with her. I always felt torn inside. I made things worse for us. Whenever I would get home and I would see your light on in your room I was like, man this is so messed up, but I was just so tired that I wouldn't go and see you," was her answer. It was hard to accept, but it was in the past, that time wouldn't be recovered. I suppose that having my bros from school served as a distraction from this mess. My mom is able to better articulate her state of mind and her emotions than she was then.

Her co-dependency affected her gravely. I didn't realize that my mom was THIS depressed until we were able to open up about our different struggles. She was struggling with being a single mom and with the breakup as well. Mom was all alone with me. Some people are strong enough to be alone and support themselves, however my mother wasn't that type. This could be partly attributed to her work hours being somewhat bizarre. She was getting in to work at two in the afternoon which meant that she wasn't making it home until past ten in the evening. I did notice that she was getting thinner and that her general mood was not the same as before, however things were apparently worse than I had perceived. So much so that, one day as I was getting back from school, I stepped into our house and there sat my two aunts and my uncle in the living room. They were my aunts, Margaret and Mary and my uncle Steven, the one named after the priest. I stepped in while they were seated on the couch, and their eyes met mine. "What's going on?", I was thinking. They had some news for me. They told me to pack my things and to get ready to leave. "Really, again?", I thought. I couldn't believe it. I saw my mother was sitting on the couch weeping next to them. When I saw her weeping it was like I knew that she was reaching a tipping point. She told me to pack my things, that I would be moving in with my Aunt Margaret and my Uncle Larry. Again it was the unknown. Why was I going away, why was she staying? I went along with it. It would grind my gears to just 'go with the flow' and it was a question that begged for an answer, but I didn't get an answer. Not yet.

CHAPTER 4

MOST (DE)FORMATIVE YEARS

I quickly did as they instructed. When you're a kid and there is no explanation for why you have to abandon everything you know, and you must simply go quickly, it makes you wonder what will happen. Your mind may wander and think so many things could be wrong but you don't have the satisfaction of an answer. If you've been there, then you understand what that feeling is like, it is a deep uncertainty. I didn't know exactly why I was going, but I suspected that things were worse off with my mom than I had known. Turns out things were worse with her. Mom was clinically depressed and she wasn't fit to care for me or even herself. I felt sad because I was leaving my mother behind and I knew that she wouldn't have anybody there to be with her at all. Nothing was sure. I was going to Flagstaff with my Aunt Margaret and Uncle Larry. He was my uncle by marriage and Aunt Margaret was my mom's oldest sister. That was all I knew. Nothing was sure, I was going to a new school and mom was staying behind by herself. Things were uncertain.

During my stay in Flagstaff mom was back home and she was having to deal with her existential crisis alone for a little bit, but she was able seek out help from a psychiatrist. Her counselor provided her with good advice and prescriptive meds to boost her mood. She was also open to talk through some of the problems that she was battling with, those many issues from her past that I had no knowledge of. She knew that the mood booster was artificial and this was helping to get her serotonin levels up, but she used the momentum to get into a better groove. She later told me when I was around, she felt so torn having to battle between seeing Joan, or not and that the only deterrent that kept her from taking her life was me. Though she wasn't there for me, deep down she really wanted to be. She is there for me now, but at the time I simply knew that she wasn't. She was doing what she could. I don't know what it is like to be a single parent, if the tables were turned would I have pulled through? Honestly, I don't know. We all know what 'we would do' if we were in someone else's shoes, but we are never in anybody else's shoes. I have to remind myself of that. When was the last time I walked in someone else's shoes? We all have a human nature, but the answer is I have never fully understood another person. Yes there a lot of single mom's out there, and we all suffer similarly to one another, but no single person has the exact same set of circumstances as another. The important thing is she reached out for help when she needed it. She was at her rope's end and she was willing to admit it. It hurt to leave her but in the long-run it was for the best.

The way it happened is she called my Aunt Margaret one day and told her, "I can't do this anymore. I am tired." That's why they had me move to Flagstaff. In speaking to her I asked her, "What was it that you meant when you said that you couldn't do THIS anymore? What did that mean at the time?" Her response to me, "I just meant that I couldn't continue like that. I don't really know if I meant life period or just keeping you there with me. I honestly don't know. I did have thoughts of suicide but I didn't want to leave you even more alone than you already were. I needed to get better so I felt at peace knowing that you would be with your aunt and uncle in Flagstaff." She was right considering all things. There are always ups and downs in our daily lives, but particularly if you are missing your only parent.

One thing to note that my mother was slowly getting better, but she wasn't the only one receiving help from a psychiatrist. When I first arrived to Flagstaff my extended family thought that it would be a good thing for me to get help due to having moved around a lot, and because of my lack of a father figure. They had also learned of the mistreatment that Joan dished out to me, this was the main reason they leaned towards seeking help for me. I remember walking into the psychiatrist's mahogany filled office. It had a nice light strawberry air freshener smell and there was a beautiful red rug on the floor. It seemed as if my life coach had enough psychology and prescriptive books to complete the psychology section in a averaged-sized library. She was in her early to mid-forties and there was something genuine about her smile. I didn't only notice her smile, but her eyes smiled as well, this is what seemed genuine. I just stayed on guard mentally as I would normally do when meeting new people. I don't remember her ice-breaker but she was such a good conversationalist. Pretty soon, a couple of sessions in, I felt comfortable enough to begin dumping my information on her. It was a rarity for me to share my insecurities. It was a way to get my interior some fresh air, just being honest for once. I shared relevant information in relation to what my family had me speaking to her in the first place. Towards the end of this session I told her something to the effect of, "I have also been lying a lot. At school I lie about who I am. I pretend to be different. You know my mom is a lesbian but I make up having a dad sometimes." I shared about being a single child and of course moving around a ton. I gave her a considerable amount of background information. She may literally be the only person that I was completely honest with in a long time leading up to that point and for a significant time after that. My story that I shared with her, had me coming from a small town, which was the honest truth. It was good to be honest for a change. Her advice was priceless, "I was adopted actually so we have SOME things in common. I lied a lot in school too, you know? You have to do what you have to do." There it was, she pretty much gave me license to keep lying. I didn't expect her to affirm me in my lifestyle. "Damn, I can keep lying." I thought to myself while being surprised. It was nice to be myself for a change. Don't get me wrong, I didn't bust out into tears in front of her at all, very few people see me cry. I yearned to be that authentic kid again, but time was passing. So many things are fleeting, but I didn't realize that all of the opportunity was around me, I just had to find them.

Once in Flagstaff I was grateful that my aunt and uncle had me at their place and it also gave me the time to get closer to my cousins. I had a lot of fun with them. Though it was nice to be there I never felt fully welcomed, I never felt at home or in my element there. I was able to slide right into the school and make friends. I stuck with my Hawaii story and all of the girls loved it. I am not tooting my own horn, however I didn't have much trouble in that area at all. While at my aunt and uncle's place, I worried for my mother's condition frequently. I hoped that she was fine. I knew she missed me. I just knew it. Sometimes I was trudging along and at other times I was doing well. It always helped to have extra encouragement.

My baptismal godmother, Aunt Mary, also lived in town so at times she would take me shopping or to catch a movie. She didn't completely lavish me with complete affection but she was always authentic and simply a genuine person with me. I enjoyed checking out the new city. I was fine with meeting people, but when I met new people it was frequently an invitation for me to become something other than I was. I even would morph a little for my uncle, whom I was living with. I joined this one sport to make him more interested in me. I figured that it would make him consider me more. I had the potential to be good at wrestling but my heart wasn't in it. I didn't want to be there much of the time. Often times I cracked jokes but I performed in the sport when I had to. While wrestling I lost most of my earlier matches. Towards the middle of the season I got noticeably better. I probably split my losses and victories fifty-fifty. While the season progressed, I made friends there rather quickly. My biggest drawback with meeting new people is that I was constantly concerned of what they would think of me. It was the same familiar tune. I needed people's validation because I didn't have that from my mother, and I felt like I had to perform for my uncle to be validated. I needed to be accepted even if that meant I couldn't be myself. I wish that I could be honest with the new students that I was being introduced to, I wished to have a realness to me. I wished for that naturalness around my aunt and uncle so I could be myself. I didn't share that with my own mother either. Mom and I have trust today, but it is still a work in progress.

I only stayed in Flagstaff for a few months. I was still the jokester and that was all me but I definitely played up some aspects of my character. I definitely played up my academics. I lied to people as usual. People either thought that my parents wanted me to go to a better school or that my dad worked a lot, given my home situation. I went with whatever 'truth' was the most convenient. It was like repeating everything all over again. It was *déjà vu* for that brief period. The girls liked me because I had a funny personality and I was always dressed well. I typically went to school with a spritz of the right cologne and I seemed supremely confident because my stories would always one-up those of the other kids. I was involved in athletics. The funny thing about the athletics, I couldn't lie my way around any of my abilities there, or rather my lack of athletic abilities. I was just an empty shell of who I truly was. It would have been nice to say what type of background I came from and still be completely myself. Of course, I wasn't aware that my family or background didn't necessarily define me. Having a lesbian mom didn't define me. Her orientation is one thing altogether, but it was the fact that we were struggling so much to be close to one another, that would have been the most difficult to share. If I had a father and a mother in a single household that wouldn't have defined me either. We can't be naive though. All of these things do color our characters and our outlook on life, but once again they don't define us. What defines us is who we are. Our actions can define us as well, because our actions eventually become who we are. I didn't quite understand this, especially since I was only wrapping up my seventh grade year.

After concluding the seventh grade my mom had me move back to Awhatukee to have me with her. She was evidently getting to a better enough state where I could live with her. When I saw her I realized that her face was fuller and her olive-toned skin had returned.

I was glad to see her. It was just us again. I was glad that it would be this way. I was happy to have my friends back. Once I had settled in with my mom and I began school again I began to make other friends among another group that seems unsuspecting, it still surprises me today. This group is the Latter Day Saints.

During the time, with all of the moving I was doing in my life, I was still searching for meaning. I wanted to grow in my life. I didn't associate this desire with my relationship to God. It didn't help that my mom never took me to church, nor did she help cultivate my love for God. I was more focused on what was right in front of me. I wanted stability and a good home. I wanted to be accepted and to belong to a community. I couldn't be blamed for that at all. That is a completely normal aspiration. My ticket in was to become Mormon. I have been around Mormons most of my life, and I have always noticed that the family is at the center of much of what they do, and at the center of their lives. I believed that they were good people, based upon my personal experience with them. I knew several Mormon people at school and they were all nice people. Among these was a nice Mormon girl in my grade, Audrey, and I realized soon that she was also a really good person. She didn't play any angles. It was also a plus that she was pretty. We all know Mormon girls are pretty, but I promise this wasn't the main reason that I eventually joined.

There general demeanor made me curious to know what they believed because they all seemed to be a closely knit community. I asked Audrey about her faith and she was eager to share it with me. Members of the Latter Day Saints that I've met typically have a deeply fostered identity rooted in their faith. She was able to get a couple of missionaries to come and visit me at my home and her father even came, which was a surprise to me. I could tell they really believed their faith. We met and greeted one another and then we talked about life a little bit. He told me that he was a lawyer. I told him I was in the eighth grade. They shared their faith with me and they gave me a Book of Mormon. I began to read the stories and I enjoyed them. It was good entertainment, I would place myself in some of the stories and imagine myself in the different scenes. They told me to pray while reading the Book of Mormon, and if I received a good burning feeling about it then I would know that it was true. I began to develop a companionship with these guys because they would visit frequently and we would discuss their religion. They would answer my questions patiently. Soon enough I plugged into their local church and I attended their version of doctrine teaching. I joined with the high school class, even though I was slightly younger. They wanted me to feel welcomed and they did a great job at that. I noted that many of the Mormons in that area were well off. Many of them were doctors, lawyers, teachers, and other types of professionals. I then decided that I wanted to become Mormon. It was wrong to want to become Mormon because of my version of the prosperity gospel, and my intention wasn't really for belief in their principles and tenets of faith. I only desired a good home. It was a hope that I was given, but it wasn't hope in God necessarily. I can honestly say that many Mormon families are prime examples of what domestic life should be like, so they gave me hope. THE lack of a true domestic life is why it was so easy for me to join up with them, and I was accepted. They made it feel like I could grow, and they did help me to grow.

I was able to compensate for my lack of a true home by hanging out with Mormon families. The Mormons that I met there were friendly and always welcoming. One example of an amazing family were the Brimhall's. I used to go over to their house for dinner, and they would give me rides over to the local ward. They were extremely nice to me, so much so, that I hoped that they would adopt me. I even almost let that slip at dinner one evening, but I had a good enough sense of propriety to not do that. I thought that this would be how I would find a good home.

Back to Akimal Middle School it was. In school I reacquainted with some of my popular friends. My friends and I had a game called bodies. We would rally up in a circle and take body shots at each other with our fists. We typically did this in the bathroom. Whoever tapped out of the game would lose. Essentially we would skip the lunch line to the very front, and we would scarf down our meals.

After we finished with lunch we would hurry to the restrooms to play our game. Sometimes we played a quick round in between periods. I was never beaten. A couple of my other buddies didn't lose either but we didn't challenge each other to a match. None of us was willing to risk our perfect win streaks. No guts no glory. There isn't much I could say about middle school life except that it was awkward. Most kids are awkward during puberty and at school it seems. That is the stigma usually, but not me. I was more so awkward at home, rather than at school. I was popular in school. I was that cool dude. My buddies and I would take our time when walking to class because it was cool to walk slow in the hallways. I listened to 50 cent, Eminem, The Game among other rap artists. I dressed nicely and I had a lot of friends. If anything I was awkward around my family. This period in Ahwatukee was short lived. I was pretty soon set to move elsewhere. I was only there a semester and my mom informed me that I would be moving again. I told her with a sigh that I didn't want to go. I was sick of moving all over the place, and I was becoming convinced that I would never be happy at home. In fact, I didn't have a home.

I conceded to my mother's request. Mom and I both longed for me to have a good family environment, but our ideas of what that was supposed to look like were different. The disconnect between our common notion was that she was my family and she acted like that wasn't enough. She made a choice and I didn't have much of one. At this point I was sick of having to make new friends, but I was moving back to Holbrook. I moved in with my Aunt Vina and Uncle Richard. It was interesting because I moved in with cousins as well and this was the first time that I would live with a large family. I had five cousins by my aunt and uncle but four of them lived there, so there was a total of seven of us under the roof. Dale had just got in from the greater Phoenix area and he and I split a room. We had bunkbeds. Then there was Joseph and Mark. Mark and I were in the same grade. We kind of clicked from the beginning. Tiffany was a sophomore in high school. Uncomfortable and fun. Those are probably the two words that I would could use most to describe this stage. I tried to make it work.

It was an interesting dynamic for me because we had to share things in common. For instance I had to share the room with Dale and it seemed to me that he didn't like me. I had infringed on his space and he didn't seem happy about that, he was never a warm person to me. He is also kind of a quiet guy, so it may just be that. So there were seven of us and it was a four bedroom and two bathroom house. It was nice though because it taught me some basic responsibilities, such as cleaning up after myself. It taught me to be mindful of other people. My Uncle Richard was fine with having me there. He did his best to reach out and be present. He was big on taking us to the park to shoot hoops which I wasn't opposed to at all. I noticed that my Aunt Vina wasn't too keen on having me there though. Maybe it had something to do with the fact that I was really hitting a growth-spurt and I was hitting the weights, so naturally I was hungry most of the time. My cousin Mark and I would walk home from school during lunch to fix up big triple-stacked sandwiches. We created a special, called the PB&J big mac, just picture that. Aunt Vina knew that chances were, if someone was rummaging through the refrigerator, it was probably me. My aunt never voiced any discomfort while I was there but it was noticeable on her face. This was the uncomfortableness that was peppered throughout my stay there. We tried to make it work.

I learned to evolve and grow. Several people in town knew who my family was and they were aware of my existence. The fun part kicks in because of my surroundings in that setting. I had lived there briefly as a kid when I was first born. The family name was pretty well known in that town of several thousand. Some people recalled having babysat me, others knew my mother, and still others knew my grandparents to be fine church-going folk. They burst my bubble before I could form it. Quickly I realized that I couldn't lie about where I was from to my peers at school. Nonetheless, I was still a fun guy and I made friends quickly despite not being able to tell people any origin story. I was no longer from Hawaii, nor could I fashion any crazy stories about my birthplace. It was a breath of fresh air though, it was still cool to be Dan the Man and be accepted. That was my nickname at school. I didn't have to hide the fact that I was born in a neighboring small town called Show Low. Relief. People accepted me for who I am, the girls still liked me, and I was relatively popular. I enjoyed just being me. I enjoyed being Daniel.

I thought my surroundings and the people around me would be a damper on my personality, on the contrary it allowed for more of my true personality to come out. This was truthfulness coupled with my cousin Mark and the fun I had with him. This doesn't mean that I didn't miss being with my mom. Though my situation with her wouldn't have been ideal, it was still something that was familiar. Living with my mom was something that I knew and missed. Mark was a good distraction from that. We had some classes together and we would meet up during lunch and head home to get a bite. Aside from all of these commonalities we had together, we were good friends. My friendship with Mark was the first true one that I had. I became more acutely aware of this because it was something good that was injected into my life. Friendship for me was like medicine for a lonely person. It had been missing. It was something that I needed.

I didn't realize how much I needed this accompaniment until I had it. My mother would visit on occasions. I was in dire need of companionship. At school I was accepted for who I was, and not by some fabrication of mine. It was a small-town school, and I actually did well there because the educational system there was a couple of notches above dismal. I in turn wished that I could also be accepted at home. I of course still missed my mother and I began to drift into a general malaise. One day Mark saw me crying, and crying was not something that I would do in front of people. I couldn't articulate what I was going through, but it was obvious I was going through a rough time. I was in a depressive mood. He promised me that high school would be better for me, that I would have a better time there. That type of encouragement can certainly make people consider their self-worth again. I was happy to have a friend like him. I grew a lot during this time but I was only just beginning. It was fun to be me and I had a friend there to help me. We played sports after school and we would go out to the movies with our friends. He was good company. It was fun, and we made it work. That is what we have to do when the unexpected comes our way, we adapt while still being ourselves. That doesn't mean to always go with the flow, though in this case I didn't have any other options.

I moved back to Pinetop with my grandparents as I was starting the ninth grade. They shared with my mother that they believed it would be better for me to live with them, and she went with it. On discussing this with her in the present day, mom says she wanted me to have good influences in my life. She should have been that influence for me from the beginning. Shoulda, coulda, woulda but we make do with the cards we are dealt. "Maybe their example would be good for you Dan", my mom remembers saying. There was somewhat of a disconnect there for a while, because they have always been good and innocent people. My grandparents, like everyone else were influenced by their surroundings, but they are the type to influence their environment in turn. I had been influenced by my environment in some negative respects, but like most kids I didn't assert myself to influence my environment. They weren't naive, they were simply too innocent to know about what I had suffered, and there is a difference. I was angry that I had to move once again, I was sad that I had to move yet another time. I had a lot of pent up emotion inside and I didn't have a healthy way to channel all of it or a way to make it subside. I was confused and I had occasional thoughts of suicide. My grandfather was always a strict guy and as a consequence, he and I butt heads often. He always had chores lined up for me to do. I couldn't ever stay up too late, but late for him was anything past nine o'clock. He told me to make sure that my bed was always made and he expected the bathroom to be spotless. I now know that he tried to instill discipline in me so that I could build character, but again it was way too much for me too soon. I thought that he hated me, simply because he was a disciplinarian. There were times we yelled at each other. My grandma today points out that she thinks we are exactly like each other. She says, just like him, I do not hesitate to tell it like it is. Grandpa and I have similar temperaments. We tend to clash with people that we are similar to so that makes a lot of sense. Some important things require reflection and introspection to notice them. Other times people point them out for us like in this case.

When I look back on my time with my grandparents I can't help but notice how impoverished I was in my attitude towards life. It was certainly difficult as it would have been for any other kid that could be in a similar situation. I was fixed in a situation that was always in flux. Very little was certain. While initially back in Pinetop-Lakeside I tried to compensate for the disconnect with my grandfather by holding onto the Mormon faith, not that I had incredible faith. Being Mormon for me wasn't really about having hope though, rather it was a commodity for me. It was strange trying to hide that from Grandpa because I knew very clearly he wasn't too fond of them. I didn't go to the Mormon Church during this time. He knew about having gone in the past, and he wasn't pleased with me about it. If I had gone, it would have been like adding insult to injury. We didn't need another thing to disagree on.

In fact, Grandpa didn't only disagree with the Mormon teachings, he didn't like Mormons at all. Aside from the cultish vibe they gave to him, he had a whole story behind his dislike for them. Turns out that as a younger man, before my mother was even born, he was moving from Phoenix to Holbrook for work at the local power plant. He was thinking about settling in a neighboring town called Joseph City, Arizona. It was populated mainly by Mormons and it was named after Joseph Smith of course. He was having a difficult time finding a suitable place. The suitable places weren't even all taken up. One day he walked into a gas station and a gentlemen asked if he was the one looking for a place in that area. Grandpa had been searching in the area for a while. He said that yes he was. The gentleman answered him pretty snidely, "You aren't going to find anything here because you are Catholic and because you are Hispanic." Though he wasn't welcomed the area, he was resolute. He eventually settled in Holbrook but he also experienced some prejudices from many Mormons in his day, so his solution was to shut them off. He says that many of them were buddy buddies with him and others at the plant when they first arrived but if they didn't convert or seem interested in their religion, they would ostracize them. He also noticed that some of them were genuinely racist. It seems like he had his reasons to feel some enmity towards Mormons, we all have a history. One word in favor of the Mormons, if you are ever in a small-town and your car breaks down, you better hope that there are some Mormons around, because they will definitely help you out. Nonetheless, my grandparents had me going to their local parish. I went along with it because at the catechesis class they offered pizza and for the girls. I went to various Masses offered for the youth. However, I still considered the Mormon lifestyle for my own-self.

Some of the Mormons in small towns had a different dynamic, they were either distinctively rich or poor, still others were in stark poverty. There was hardly a happy medium. It was my usual agenda, I needed a ticket out. However, their beliefs to me were becoming increasingly harder to stomach and I was becoming a little skeptical of them. I didn't risk going to their church. There was no way I would let my grandparent find out that I was taking active steps to becoming a Mormon. I was actually an initiated Mormon at one point. I always admired them though, for their nice family life. I still admire them for that. They helped ease my life, which was always so transitory.

Soon I was introduced to a traveling missionary named Brandon, whom was of the catholic-charismatic type. He had his home in Pinetop-Lakeside. He was genuine and on fire for his faith. I had never met a Catholic like him before, someone so rooted in his belief in Christ, as a Catholic! He was somewhat influential in my life. Brandon asserted a positive attitude and he was outgoing. I began to get more interested in Catholicism again. He didn't debunk Mormonism, so much as present me with the coherence of Catholicism. He showed me the reasoning behind believing Catholicism, both scripturally and historically. He answered my questions whenever I had them. I did a renouncement of Mormonism and I no longer believed it. I no longer saw the truth in it. I will note that, even though I held one religion as true, it didn't mean that other religions didn't have truth in them. My conclusion was that

Mormonism wasn't for me. I still had a longing for a family and all of those good things, but I wanted to understand and know the truth. After having met Brandon I was more hesitant to accept just anything at face value. I was turning over a new leaf, but this new leaf was not a withering one, but one that was very much alive. I would only discover this further on down the road. There was still so much struggle to occur before that could happen.

Grandpa and I clashed so much that after a year of living with them, I told my mother that I wanted to move back in with her. I was very unhappy living with my grandparents because all of the tension. I moved back to Phoenix with my mother. It was a big problem for me to keep moving from one place to another as a hot potato jumps from one hand to another, and I had no say in it. I have strong opinions and desires. As an effect of this, I have not been the guy to just go with the flow. That disposition isn't natural to me. I didn't understand this then, but it was important for me make the choice to move back to my mom's. Little did I know that the grass wasn't necessarily greener.

Once I was back at home with my mom I was excited to move back to the valley, to be back in the big city. I thought that my mother had changed maybe. Some people would call me naive but I was only an adolescent and I was hopeful for the better. It wouldn't have helped to have been cynical, but for many people that would have been their initial expectation. I soon realized that my mother would occasionally see Joan still and I thought to myself, "Really? - man you haven't changed." Hope wasn't stifled but it was definitely a blow. I still held onto the my Catholic faith. I was returning to it, but it wasn't easy. I could still hold on to hope, sometimes that is all we have. What is hope if there aren't thorns and thistles to make it worthwhile? I didn't understand the value of this lesson at the time, but I would begin to understand in Phoenix.

It was summer time before the tenth grade and these lessons of struggle and hope didn't register for me. It was nearly impossible for them to sink in because I was forced to deal with being let down by mom constantly. She was still seeing Joan and I was on the back burner again. I resented her. My grandparents were well intentioned to have me move in with them but their lifestyle was too much too soon. I had to go with the flow but this wasn't my style. I think that many adolescents with a similar childhood background just learn to assimilate the 'go with the flow' personality, but something inside of me refused to do that. Do not misinterpret, one of my best friends today is a 'go with the flow' type of guy and it can work fine for people, but it is not me and it never has been me. We need these people in the world, but I emphasize that's not me. My strong opinions and desires were being hurt because of my mother's decision to keep seeing Joan. I also had to face the reality that my mom had issues. After a while I thought her instances of putting me on the back burner would stop once her outings with Joan began to dwindle. I was sorely wrong, many instances more were to come. Hope in life is worthwhile, but what is so difficult about hope is that we hope for things we cannot see. Though, for hope to be worthwhile, it requires thorns and thistles.

CHAPTER 5

UNRECOGNIZED, UNHEARD, UNSEEN

I will not pretend to have the greatest hope. From an objective standpoint I probably should have given up the hope that a relationship with my mom could be salvaged, but hope is crazy like that. I hoped even when there weren't grounds to hope any longer. Hope doesn't betray us, the circumstances do, fate betrays us, but not hope. Some people give up hope, when hope seems nonsensical. This was not the case with me, at this point I had grown, I was evolving. I was in high school and I was beginning to question my place in the world. I was beginning to wonder why I was meant to be on this earth. I was going into the tenth grade and I was happy to move in with my mom again. "Things would surely be different now", I thought to myself. Hope gave me surety. My mother had just acquired a new condo which had two bedrooms and two bathrooms in South Phoenix. We would be living there together, just the two of us. The loan she acquired for the condo was from Bank of America. She, like many other Americans, shouldn't have even been approved for these loans in the first place. They did not qualify for them. Later on this affected us when the house market crashed and the recession hit. Mom had to work extra hours because we were barely living within our means. I knew that my mother had ended her romantic relationship with Joan previously because she called my mom a cunt. They still saw each other periodically even after such a distasteful remark. One day they were speaking on the phone and Joan asked my mom, rather pointedly, if my mom missed her. My mother realized for the second time that she was no longer co-dependent on Joan and that she really didn't miss her. "No," was my mom's reply. Joan became angry and she began yelling and cussing her out. My mother didn't even respond, she hung up and that was that. She was finished with Joan for good.

Mom began to see her own mistakes it seems, but she wasn't to the point of admitting them yet. However, she has gotten better at articulating her thoughts and feelings since. Mom knew that I would be writing this book so she decided to write a letter about her thoughts on Joan. Today she has a more honest take on herself and she is more aware of our past situation.

> *Dear Joan,*
> *Are you happy now? Your anger, blame abuse, caused my son and I pain and anguish. You belittled us for so long. You were a complete bitch, Oh yes, and you used me also. Is there hope for you? There is always hope. Although, I don't know if you can ever come out of yourself without serious help. I don't know if you are evil. The vile things that come out of your mouth would suggest that. I never loved you. My opinion of myself was so low that I lowered myself to be with you. I was beyond paralyzed, emotionally and physically. I haven't seen your face in 15 years and I could go another 150 years not seeing you. So, Joan are you happy now?*

She was finally done with Joan, and that door was shut but the damage had been done. Once I was aware of that their relationship had ended, I imagined that we could really connect now. We did connect, only briefly. We went to the movie theatre at times, we would eat out some, or just talk at home. It wasn't so much the activities that we did as it was the time spent together that was great. Before I came back, Mom told me that she wanted everything to be perfect for me. Seemingly they were, but it was so brief, I needed love and attention.

The love and attention that I warranted was not given to me. Sometimes for relationships to work all that is needed is pure unrestricted time. One of the biggest killers to any type of relationship is to say, I don't have time. It reads and sounds exactly as we say it — "I don't have time for you now." These relationship killers were ever present and that was the constant, the variable was always in what shape this relationship killer would come in. Mom met a friend of Joan's named Brandi. You might say that any of my mom's partners were an intrusion on me being treated like a son, and a detriment to my mom fulfilling her role as my mom. So the time spent away from work that we could have had together wasn't meant for me. I was faceless, voiceless, and unrecognized. She was getting to know Brandi a bit more but it was sort of a fling. They didn't last long and Brandi eventually moved away. My impression of her is that she was an irrational person. She seemed psycho and it wasn't simply that I was cynical, I genuinely believe that she had mental issues, diagnosed or otherwise. To my credit there were times in which Brandi tried to convince my mother that I had mental issues. She was extremely manipulative. I was struggling with depression and I tried to communicate this to my mom, and Brandi would tell her that I should be taken to jail or to a mental institution. My mother never stood up for me and she possibly may have considered Brandi's suggestions.

After this entire ordeal my mom was single for a little while and she would bond with her co-worker Lidia. Lidia is that typical butch lesbian woman who wore Carhartt boots, work jeans, and flannels. She has a lively personality. In fact, my mom and Lidia are still friends today. I will note that her story varies greatly from my mom's own story. I had the opportunity to speak with her about it, and I think it is noteworthy because it clarified a couple of things on homosexuality for me, especially what being lesbian is like.

When I was a bit older, around sixteen years old, I was hanging out with mom at Lidia's place. We were outside on the front porch and Lidia and I were speaking about general things in life. At the time I was in high school and I was pretty inquisitive, especially when others were open to conversation. I still carry this characteristic today.

"Do you have a girlfriend?" she asked curiously.

"I've got a couple actually," I stated with a grin and while nodding my head. "Oh Casanova here! What are their names?" she asked with amusement in her voice.

"Let me run through my rolodex, well my number one is Melissa, and the other one is Shaniqua." We laughed about it.

I was curious and I couldn't help myself so I asked her, "So…like, have you always been lesbian?"

Without reservations, she answered very naturally, "Yeah, I have."

"Oh wow, you mean since you were a kid?" I asked her.

"Yeah, I've always felt an attraction for girls and I've always felt like a boy inside, but I mean that's just me personally. I even felt uncomfortable going into the women's bathroom as a kid. It didn't seem right." she added.

"Oh wow, that is crazy," I replied.

I was surprised that she would know that much about herself at such a young age. I found that to be interesting, I couldn't place myself in her shoes but I was intrigued to hear her story. I asked other questions about her sexuality and she was open to answer. Upon reflecting on her story I could see some fast distinctions between my mom's story and Lidia's. The first being, Lidia knew that she was homosexual ever since she was a kid, and that she was born homosexual. Her story stands in direct contrast to my mom's story. I was offered an alternative narrative to my own, and I couldn't help but be intrigued.

That is why it is important to understand other people's views and experiences as best we can. Our experiences sum up reality for each of us as individuals in a subjective sense, but it doesn't sum up reality in general. My mom, on the other hand, slowly discovered this about herself. She told me about an encounter she had with another woman when she was twenty-six and I was two. This was during her drumming and partying days. It was after the encounter that she finally connected the dots. As a kid she was always a tomboy, but it didn't mean anything to her then. Eventually she was abused as a kid and she had a deep mistrust for men. When she finally did trust a man, he abandoned her while she was expecting their son. The next guy was a fling, but she always felt emotionally connected to women rather than men. It then hit her that she liked women and that was the route she was going to take. My mom's discovering of her homosexual orientation was a drawn-out development and it brought confusion to her at times. Lidia was different, she was always sure that she liked the same sex.

I remember always liking how warm and friendly Lidia was. It wasn't so much that I didn't like homosexual people, because I don't dislike any group of people, but there are certainly things that I don't agree with. It was difficult for me though, because she is my mother and as a result I couldn't have the type of home that I would have liked. I saw my grandparents example and that was what I wanted for us. My mother's love life wasn't ever a big matter to me because I didn't care much for her partners, but it had to be important to me because it affected me so directly. I had some stake in it all.

The way that Lidia factors into all of this is that she introduced my mom to her sister Yaritza, another Safeway employee. I don't doubt that people who are homosexually oriented can genuinely love other people in the broadest sense, or romantically as well, but my mom's involvement with Yaritza was different. Yaritza and my mother met and they liked each other from the beginning, but liking someone can change so suddenly. I don't think I would venture to call it love, however.

They began to see each other. In a week's time they were officially dating. They saw each other almost daily. The crazy thing was that my mom always had to pay for their outings. Lidia warned my mother about Yaritza, because she had a tendency to be a moocher. My mom and Yaritza were moving fast. One day suddenly as I stepped into the condo I see Yaritza and her three kids in the living room with my mom. The oldest child was a freshmen, and the next two were in the sixth and the fifth grades respectively. I did the formality and said hello, I then walked to the refrigerator hoping to be inspired by something I saw. I opened the door and I pondered as the light hit my face, "Mmmm…What do we have here? Hot Pockets? No, I had that yesterday. What about the beef and bean burrito? I am sick of those. Ooh, microwavable pizzas! There we go." I thought to myself as I finally made up my mind. I popped them into the microwave as I went straight to my room. I got on my computer and logged into MSN messenger, MySpace. The night was spent and before I knew it, I was waking up the next day. I began to get ready for school and I realized that they had all spent the night. I didn't think anything of it, I had spent some nights at Brandi's place when my mom was dating her so this seemed normal. I got ready and went to school. I had a long boring day at school and then I swung by taco bell with my friends. I saw that they we there again. This happened for a few more days and as it was occurring I notice more of their things accumulating all over our place. The bathroom was becoming a mess. "What the fuck is going on?", I said as more of an exclamation than a question to my mom. "Do they live with us?" I asked my mom. "Yeah," she answered casually. "Well tell them to leave!," I exclaimed. Her response was entirely too casual, "I can't do that." I couldn't believe it. "Yes you can, it's our house," I argued. She refused to tell them to leave and I was angry about this. She let Yaritza walk all over her and I was fearful that it would be another case of Joan all over again. I would have to try to make the best of it. It is honestly a blur how long they stayed at the condo because I tried to busy myself outside of school to avoid spending time at the condo. I felt faceless, voiceless, and unrecognized. I would soon realize that this was very much the case at home, and there wasn't much I could do except avoid being home. I would eventually break new ground and begin to come into my own element, but with much help.

I had my methods of staying away from home. I would start my day by begrudgingly going to school because I had to. I never thought of quitting and I did realize that I needed a high school diploma, but that was my attitude towards it, I had to get through it. I did enough to be barely above passing. I was apathetic towards school, I didn't even care to see my friends. In fact, I had not even the slightest desire to make friends. I actually avoided making friends. I wasn't popular and I had lost the concern of what people made of me. Inside I felt dead and I was probably just another faceless silhouette marching the hallways to the next class. The bell would ring and it was just mechanics from thereon out. The only exceptions were some of my high school teachers and the counselors there. During my studies they were a great encouragement for me. Several girls liked me and they were into me, but I didn't take them seriously. I did hang out with some of them and we would go on casual dates sometimes, but I was not my best self. I hooked up with a few of them. What a quick way to destroy a friendship. It goes both ways, it takes two to tango. Besides, in my mind no one could replace my original crush, Tapenga from Boy Meets World, she was always number one. Aside from the occasional love conquest at school, I still excelled in subjects that involved history and geography. At this point however, my love for history was like a hobby. It is not until later that my hobby for informally studying history proves to be a significant portion of my life. As long as I was away from home, then I could be calm and collected. History and geography were a great way for me to imagine myself someplace else.

I began to work at Arizona Mills Mall during the week after school. My mother couldn't take me to work because she would often have her car commandeered by Yaritza, because she had to take her kids somewhere all of the time. Seems she all she needed was a place to crash while she carried on with her listless life. I wasn't motivated in any way except for the desire to leave that place. Late in my sophomore year and in the beginning of my junior year I began working at the mall, and I would take the city bus there. It is there that I begin to meet many people from different nationalities and from all over the world. It was as if I had escaped from my situation at home, this was my avenue for learning about new cultures. One thing that I have noticed is that many people from foreign countries tend to have a warm disposition. I can almost always spot a foreigner based solely upon his demeanor. Many foreigners have an innate disposition for camaraderie and bonding that I don't find much in the West. This was attractive to me.

At work I was having regular conversations with Israelis, Palestinians, and the Turkish. I was expanding my knowledge and openness to other people. Our conversations revolved around their respective homelands. I was actually keeping up with them and I was becoming informed. It wasn't just small talk, I was authentically interested in what they had to say. That as a result for them was refreshing. Whenever I asked the question, "Where are you from?", it was a question that held weight. I wouldn't ask it for the sake of asking it, I was genuinely interested. Neither my question nor their responses were stale. I would practice greetings, common phrases, jokes, and cuss words with them. They were always impressed by my ear for the phonetics. Chances were if I was given a phoneme or a word to pronounce, I could handle it. Soon I was very passionate about learning Turkish. That was the language that I was most eager to practice. It was the most accessible language for me and the people were very open. I began to pick it up so it became more logical for me to continue learning it. I got on a website called LiveMocha to get connected with people from all over the world to learn other languages. I did eventually do some studying of Portuguese and Turkish before one of my future travels, but at the moment I was extremely drawn to Turkish. I listened to Turkish music and I even bought some books in Turkish to improve my skills and pronunciation. This was the first time I had to face my cultural identity. Whenever people asked me what my ethnic background was or what my heritage was, I would always say that I was Hispanic. It was a neat time. I began to grow by meeting new people and this was coaxing me out of my own self and helping me to be comfortable with myself around other people.

I also had begun to attend a Catholic Church in my vicinity that was associated with the *Miles Jesu* community. Their name means Soldier of Jesus in Latin. They were comprised of two priests and five brothers. I used to take the bus down to the location and I began to attend the Mass there on the weekends. Sometimes I would also frequent it during the week. It was so beautiful to go to the liturgy and I always felt at home at that particular church. I had my grandparents,

I sort of had my mother, and friends came and went, but in reality the only consistent thing in my life has been my pursuit of knowledge about God, even though I didn't care for him at times. God was always in the back of my mind. My grandparents can most definitely take the credit for this impact in my life.

The people at *Miles Jesu* were very warm and welcoming. I noticed it then but I have become more away of this now. I was like an ant in the ant-farm, in the middle of everything, but with some reflection and with taking a step back, things are much clearer. I just needed a Catholic Church that was nearby and that was it. What kept me going to this church is that the people's lifestyles were very attractive. They were simple men but they were educated. The priests and the brothers spoke English, Spanish, and some Italian. I would go to Mass and then talk to the church goers afterwards. They welcomed me with open arms. I eventually plugged in enough and I would do little tasks, such as helping with some of their maintenance. The cool thing is that they all treated me like an adult. I did imagine that they could guess my home situation was not ideal because they never saw a parent drop me off at the church and I never brought my mom up in conversation. They weren't judgmental people. It was at this time that I began to have thoughts about the priesthood, but I didn't take them all to seriously. These thoughts would be in the back of my mind for a while. These two places, learning Turkish at work and praying at church, were refuges for me from both my home and school. They couldn't last forever and I did have to go home at the end of the day. I had to eventually face the situation at home. So I tried to do that.

The limited time that I spent at home, a significant portion of it I spent arguing with my mom. My biggest point of contention with my mom was that Yaritza and her children would constantly use up all of our stuff. We didn't have any wiggle room in the house. I still cannot understand why my mom let this happen. I mean, they just showed up and forgot to leave. My mom and Yaritza never talked about it. It just happened. She had stuffed my mom's closet full of canned foods and other non-perishable items. She may have been on welfare, because at the first of the month we would spontaneously have a ton of food. Yaritza was never mean to my mom or to me, but she was simply a shitty person. Since I didn't really care about having friends I didn't have an incentive to lie to people at school. That was something I began to dislike in other people, the lying. Yaritza would blow things out of proportion the same way I had done when I was a kid. She used to claim to be a very devout Christian and I didn't see her go to church nor did she read the Scriptures, ever. She never prayed before or after meals, but that is just knit picking on my part. Let's look at some real evidence. She lied often and the reason why I didn't like her lying to us is because she was an adult with children. There were differences between us. Maybe I didn't want to grow up the same, way so it was easy to see how unappealing this trait truly was.

Some things are much different she we are on the receiving end. It may have helped me in some capacity to have been subjected to this predicament. I was the one who used to lie to everyone else just to get a leg up. It was a mini wakeup call, I didn't want to grow up being dishonest about my life all of the time. There are differences between people who have a personal and private life and those who have a secret life. It is not just semantics, to say that is simply dismissive. Yaritza lied about things that she had no reason to lie. She would outright make things up, for instance she pretended to be a person enthused with doing mission work abroad. I arrived one day after school and I found her looking at the globe we had in the apartment. Almost as soon as I stepped in she set it down and went into the kitchen where my mom was at. I then heard her tell my mom that she had done several mission trips all over Latin America. Then they glossed over the idea of Yaritza taking my mom to a couple of the places she mentioned, among were Colombia, Argentina, and Brazil. I didn't believe her so I asked her where she went to in Colombia. She didn't 'remember.' Since apparently her last mission trip was to Brazil I asked where she went to. She responded that she went to the Amazon in Rio de Janeiro. "Whaaaat!" I responded with notable disbelief. I had a map in my room and I showed her that was not possible because the Amazon forest is nowhere near

Rio. I wouldn't have believed her in anyway, but I would have been surprised if she could name one place in the Amazonas state in Brazil, Manaus for instance. I readily let her know that Rio de Janeiro was constituted of beaches and shantytown like communities called favelas. She answered me, "Oh, yeah that is where we went, the Amazonas," as if agreeing with what I just said. My mom interjected and said that Yaritza would be taking her there someday, I thought to myself, "Yeah right." My mom has matured much and is no longer as gullible. "Love you mom!" I say this today with love. We can joke together now, and be honest with ourselves, it is liberating. Aside from this type of behavior, I also resented the fact that my mother would completely disregard my opinion about just any matter. I had told my mom for years that she should quit her angel readings and her angel cards because they weren't good for her spiritually. She wouldn't provide a counterargument and she would just ignore me. Yaritza told her to quit them one day, and since Yaritza is such a 'stellar Christian ', mom quit at the drop of a dime. What disbelief…. Could I hope to be number one in my mother's book ever? I thought maybe never, but I dared to hope. Hope is a crazy thing, especially when you feel unnoticed. There was little indication that let me know it was okay to hope.

I am sure my mother wanted to be a good parent, she probably hoped for it as well. Her issue was placing bad relationships ahead of us. If you are subjecting your children to being on the back burner for a person that you know is not worth the trouble, don't! I am not saying this because my mom is gay, but her big issue was co-dependence. Her sexuality is another topic all together, but I can't control that either. Back to her codependency, I felt faceless with her. I was always on the back burner wondering if she will ever get to me. I wasn't certain anymore, but didn't I hope for it?

Yes I did, but it was painful. One movie that I think captures this notion is Shawshank Redemption. Morgan Freeman's character says that hope will drive a man crazy, especially in a place like this (the movie characters were in prison). I was stuck in this shitty situation at home. We rarely bonded, and it was particularly tough because I knew what healthy households looked like. I saw how families laughed with each other, I saw how they shared with one another. My grandparents were a prime example of what Christian understanding and of what forbearance looks like. They were always joyful people. That is not to say they haven't had their fair share of problems, but their faith has always gotten them through everything. Their faith was never a crutch but rather the mortar and foundation that supports them through thick and thin. I saw the disparity between their example and my own reality with mom. I wanted that, whatever my grandparents had, that is what I still hope for to this day. I yearned for what they had, but something so beautiful and so precious doesn't just fall out of the sky. It requires a lot of work. My grandparents are the reason why I still have Christian values and why I still went to Mass. It was the only hope I had so had to cling to it. This was all the hope that I needed, so I held onto it. That is the curious thing about hope is that the longer we hold onto it, the longer it is tried and tested, but the reward is that much sweeter.

I held onto hope but it had to be tried because then I would know how true my hope was. I fell in a deep depressive mood because of my situation at home despite the peace and harmony that I encountered at church. Much of me inside was just stripped out. I didn't care to make friends at school and I was set to conclude my junior year but I wasn't thinking of what I would be doing after high school. I didn't have goals and I lived sort of a listless life. This is the case with so many other high school students I lacked structure throughout my senior year. I slept when I wanted but I began to develop my night-owl sleep pattern, which really meant that I didn't have a regular sleep pattern. I was just squeaking by at some times but I was making it. I was so empty inside but I still kept going to Mass, even though sometimes I was just going through the motions. Sometimes in life that is all that is required of us, for us to just show up and be there.

I did show up, but my main passion and my most concrete outlet at the time was learning other languages, and learning about other cultures. I kept revisiting LiveMocha and I kept expanding my knowledge and understanding of the world. I learned whatever I could about the world because I would imagine myself moving to any number of places. I thought of being far away and not coming back. I had to get a fresh start. It was nice to fantasize about this, but I eventually had to return to reality and things at home were always a mess.

Was there time to dream when things at home stifle these same dreams? Sure there was. I kept fantasizing about leaving my problems behind and the next few weeks at home only affirmed my sentiment. I was used to having to take the city bus to go anywhere because mom would hardly ever have the car. The exception would be for her work. This was the case until one day I saw a relatively new car parked outside, so I thought maybe we had a guest over. When I saw no one else inside I asked who's car that was and Yaritza said it belonged to her. "Oh, that's a nice car Yaritza." I responded dismissively. She agreed with me. I decided to ask my mom how it was that Yaritza afforded that vehicle especially with her three children. My mom told me that she co-signed for it. I thought that my mom was out of her mind. She already had the pressure of paying her dues on the condo and if Yaritza were to miss a payment on that car, then what were we to do? Lunacy. Bank of America should never have approved her for the loan because she did not qualify for it, she and thousands of other Americans across the country alike. We were about to have the rug pulled out from under us. It was the fault of several representatives from Bank of America. The value was depreciating and her monthly loan payment was upwards of eight hundred dollars. At one point she was up to a thousand dollars a month. My mother and Yaritza broke up and it wasn't even three months after the fact that Yaritza was unable to keep up with the car payments, and they became delinquent as well. Shortly after the car was repossessed mom had to file for bankruptcy. Even I became stressed. I tried coping with all of these issues at home by hanging out with some of the chicks from school and since it was very natural to me, I hooked up with them. It was an easy escape, but I was so empty inside. I also felt conflicted because of what Catholicism says about premarital sex. My rationale was that my mom wasn't married, but she hooked up with women so I wasn't doing anything wrong or out of the ordinary. It was my senior year finally, and I wasn't even excited for it. I was so uncertain, it was the uncertainty that was the most difficult part to cope with.

It was the usual with my senior year, I went simply because it was the thing to do, to get a diploma and be done. What really got me through was attending church. I was glad that I kept going to Mass because I would draw from the peace that I got there. I had received more encouragement in my academics then I did before from some caring people. The two counselors at the beginning of the school year asked me what it was that I wanted to do once I graduated. Initially I thought of the Catholic priesthood. I sort of brushed this idea off throughout the school year but I kept it in the back of my mind. Many of my teachers wanted to see me succeed. I wanted this as well, but what does that actually look like? To succeed in life? As they were getting me to think about a career path, I was faced with so many possibilities about what to do after graduation. As my senior year concluded and I graduated, I was still trying to figure things out. I still had that longing to leave and discover more of the world. I wanted to be as far removed from my life as I could be, so I searched frantically. I wasn't in college, but I was attempting to embark on a journey. My mother had moved away from home for a year and it proved to be a valuable experience for her. I was considering the exact same thing, but I was shooting in the dark with this one.

I didn't know exactly what I would do but my intention was to go abroad. To move away and to not come back. My research wasn't the most ingenious but it worked, I just typed "how to make money abroad" in the web browser for options. The thing that popped up the most was to teach English in a foreign country. I found a TOEFL certification program that I could complete to be able to teach in a couple of settings. I researched some of these places and Argentina really caught my eye. The plan was to complete the certification program down there and teach during the evenings. I believed that I could do it. I knew a person there, my friend Pablo, from the LiveMocha website. After some research I appreciated the richness that Argentina possesses. I was settled on

Argentina. I had some money saved up from working during school. I was so convinced that this is what I wanted. I wouldn't know for sure unless I went down to Argentina to try it out. So I was determined, I was meant to leave Arizona and go to Argentina.

I was so meticulous that I planned my move in very much detail. I bought a one way plane ticket to Argentina. I created an itinerary for the first month that I would be there. I connected online with Pablo so that he could help show me around his city. So many big things to come along. I was meant to teach for an agency, that was sponsored through the TOEFL program for several months. The program was put on by people from South Africa. I even bought a new wardrobe to cope with the frigid temperatures down there. Once everything was in place my grandparents threw me a sending away party a week before I was to move away. A week later we were standing at the airport and my mother was bawling her eyes out. I am not the most sensitive guy but I cried as well. I said my goodbyes and see you laters to my mother and my grandparents. We embraced and it was so intense. Once we let go it was the determination to discover myself and to discover the world that had me continue on.

It was my launching off. My mother had a tough time letting me go, but she wanted me to go out and discover myself. She describes her experience in her own words. I knew it was difficult for her but it is only in conversation that we have come to understand each other much better. Mom explains her thoughts and feelings,

"Dan leaving to Argentina broke me. It broke me because I was losing my son. It felt exactly like this. I was stripped emotionally. How could I have this happen? I was wailing and weeping on the ground. I lost so many opportunities to be generous with him, those opportunities that will never be recovered. When will I see him smile again, when will I hear his loud laughter again? The next day I heard from him and I was more at ease. The condo I was living in was so different, so quiet without any life. My life was different without my son's presence, and still is today. When he got back, I was so happy and over-joyed to see him. But I was also declaring bankruptcy and losing my condo. I was always in some kind of upheaval and I thought, is this really me? Somewhere I lost the true me. When I had my son, I vowed to love and protect my son with everything I had and I completely failed terribly. Things had to change. I can't turn back the hands of time, so I can't change the situation but I can change my attitude. I had to change. I was going to change."

I gathered my things and I marched forward. Once I got passed security my heart sank. It hadn't dawned on me what I was doing. I planned the trip but in executing my plan it became so crazy. I was exhilarated, nervous, sad, and uncertain all at the same time. I boarded the plane and we took off, bound for the Southern Hemisphere.

Once in the sky I began to think to myself, "wow I am actually doing this." This was only my second plane trip and I was now flying from PHX - LAX to Bogota - Buenos Aires. I had a four hour layover there and the people there were very warm, expressive, and cordial. I connected to the next flight and I arrived at Buenos Aires, Argentina. It was a red-eye flight so I arrived early in the morning. Shortly after touching down I gathered my luggage and as I look back, my guardian angel must have been protecting me. Everything went so smoothly. I took a transportation service which was provided through the education program. They drove me to my quarters and turns out that the airport is not near the city. During my drive I was in awe. I had so much to learn.

Culture shock! I stepped outside once we had arrived and I could hear the city speaking to me. "Dude! I'm in Argentina!", I thought to myself. The city was so alive. I hit the block on foot. I didn't want to get lost so I made a couple of loops more. I was exhausted so I told myself that I had to check out at least one place before retiring to bed. It was chilly and I was breathing in deeply, just savoring the city. I also got a nice meal and then crashed in my room. After my nap I headed over to the school where I would be working. I walked everywhere. The city was bustling, but the people were all so friendly. Once I arrived I introduced myself to the staff and to the several people that I would be working with. I met new faces from Mexico, Switzerland, and Ireland. Every one of my colleagues spoke Spanish.

I then realized how much work my Spanish really needed. It was a good first day. I walked back home and washed up for dinner. Dinner was characteristically late, typically at ten at night, and I would be getting ready for bed near midnight or at one o'clock. I would recall the day before sleeping. It was during this night as I lied down to fall asleep, while the city was also beginning to slumber, that I began to have a broader and more in depth outlook on myself and my life.

I couldn't focus on that very much at first. I was going to be busy. Now to get through the program. I knew that I had to apply myself but it quickly became evident to me that my interrupted education was slowing me down. That was the attitude that I had though, that I was being slowed down but I would not let it impede me from accomplishing my goal. If I weren't interested in the program I wouldn't have gotten through, I had the drive. Just above barely passing, I was able to attain my certification in a matter of a month. I learned during the day and I taught some by night. Now I was freed up to dedicate more time to the craft and to exploration. I could dedicate more time to self-discovery.

Soon work began full-force and I started to teach English to students of all ages. My daily routine required a fifteen minute walk to class but the chilly weather was an antidote to my sleepyhead, I will add that I am not a morning person so it helped. I didn't mind the walk unless I was hungover from the previous night. I would work diligently during the day, and mingle with my coworkers. Several times throughout my stint there, I would hang out with my colleagues at bars or we would go to the most lit parties in town. Buenos Aires has a big draw from different parts of the country, such as Patagonia or Mendoza. There are also many Brazilians there and we had fun at different shows where well-known DJs would perform. The other foreigners and I would go out and dance often. It was weird to think that I was now a foreigner. I spent some nights reflecting on this fact and on how I was doing at teaching English. I was doing decently, but I needed to explore more of Argentina to expand my opportunity to build clientele and to understand more of the country. I stayed in Buenos Aires for a month and three weeks but since I had originally planned to teach in Rosario, I would have to make it out there eventually. Rosario is a smaller city and I had established a connection with Pablo. Once there, I met up with him and he showed me around during my down time from teaching. It is bit of a boring city and everything can be seen and ventured within four days' time. The only places that stuck out to me were the flag memorial and the Catholic cathedral in town. The latter being the place most conducive for introspection.

I reflected more on my faith, I reflected more on home, and I reflected on my future path, and on what type of work I wanted to do. One night after a long day at work I stood outside in the brisk evening and I gazed at the stars. I realized how little I was. It was the same sky back home but I was half a world away from my mom. I was so far from my grandparents. Then I realized how much I needed them. I felt as if they didn't remember me. I didn't think anyone loved me truly. The idea which led me to move across the globe from my loved ones was independence. I also tried to find fulfillment all on my own, but the truth is we need each other. I had to reconnect with my loved ones. I called them on a landline and we spoke about how they were doing and how I was fairing in the new environment. They were always supportive of my decision to either stay or to come back home, but my grandparents would have preferred me to come back right away. Things weren't so simple. I did go to church but the new city, the new job opportunity, the new lifestyle there didn't cut it for me. I was looking to be fulfilled in another way. What was I looking for? I wanted, not only an adventure, but a true journey. These things were on my heart and I had to address them but the more practical matters had to come first. At this point my money was low and I needed to head back to the city to find more work and more students so that I would be able to make it. That was a significant night for me. I headed back to Buenos Aires soon after to keep teaching. I had made up my mind to head back to Arizona, but I needed to complete my assignment.

Mom tells me that it was after I had moved from Arizona that she was able to break her co-dependency and heal from it. That she was now able to be comfortable enough in her own skin to not need a romantic relationship in her life to fill her. Towards the end of my assignment in Argentina she even communicated to me then that she wanted to make me the top priority in her life. I was excited to hear this news though my past experience let me know to not be so excited, to be more realistic with my expectations. A healthy skepticism, if you will. I finished my last assignment and within a matter of days I was on a flight that was heading back to Phoenix, Arizona. I went to stay at my grandparent's in Holbrook once I arrived. I felt like a failure because I didn't make it in the new city and I was back to square one. It was a neat experience and one that I will treasure for the rest of my life, but it was difficult one. My absence from my mother's home set some pieces in motion which would bring change for the both of us.

I searched for different career opportunities once I was back home. I took a substitution teacher job at the local school for grades kindergarten through the twelfth grade. Shortly after, I realized that I was not the best teacher, and this was largely due to my lack of a solid education, nor was I passionate about it. It was plain and simple. I still felt like a failure and the pain from coming back home was still fresh, when one day my grandparents were visited by my Uncle Larry and Aunt Margaret. I was on my way out when my uncle sat me down outside and asked why I had returned home. I responded that I missed my family and I wanted to come back. That was a weighted answer but he didn't understand how much weight it really held for me. He said that I shouldn't have returned, that I should have kept at it in Argentina. He was disappointed and mad at me for returning. I listened to what he had to say then I reflected on his words for a moment. I was more frustrated that I was back and I wasn't sure what direction to turn to. I continued to go to Mass with my grand-folks and I sought the answer to my question. I prayed about it often.

The thought of priesthood entered my mind and I was surprised how forceful the draw to it was. I began to read more of John Paul II's different writings, and I really enjoyed exploring his thoughts on personalism. I also began to do research on the Catholic priesthood and I spoke to the parish pastor about it. I sincerely hoped to find an answer and I hoped that God could let me know in an audible way, however God doesn't generally operate on our terms. I thought about the priesthood more often so I contacted the vocations director for my diocese. The vocations director of a diocese is the priest in charge of fostering priestly vocations and overseeing the seminarians in that same diocese. Seminarians are the men who enter priestly formation and studies for a particular diocese. I spoke with my vocations director a couple of times and I talked about the possibility of the priesthood with him on the phone and eventually things became more concrete. He decided to take it upon himself to come and visit me in Holbrook and meet with me face to face. I wasn't sure if this meant that I should become a priest but it was definitely a positive sign for me. This was a question that I needed to be open to in order to discover myself. There is a quote from John Paul II that I discovered that resonated with me as I began to consider this path, "The future begins today, NOT tomorrow." This was a momentous adventure that would also help me heal from my past and help me in focusing towards my present situation, and of course, my future.

CHAPTER 6

CATHOLIC PRIESTHOOD?

A Catholic priest once told me that today is closer to eternity than tomorrow will ever be. In other words, today is what really counts. It is true because tomorrow doesn't exist yet, and yesterday is long gone. This first has not yet been conceived, it has not yet become true for us. The latter once was, and is now only a memory. Today is what counts and it has taken me a long time to realize this, I sometimes still forget. I was very anxious to know whether I was meant to be a priest or not. I was anxious to know whether it was what I truly wanted in my life. When I began to explore this possibility, I begin my own existential quest. What can I do for the rest of my life, without losing who I am in my core? I was also anxious to know what God wanted for me. I also considered priesthood by default because as kid I was very drawn to it. Being a priest was the first thing I wanted to do with my life. When I was a child I played my mock-Masses and I would try to get my cousins to participate. I had more than an appreciation for it, I was very inclined towards the religious ever since I was a kid. It was always in the back of my mind, but is it as simple as choosing one? It was sometimes tough to consider giving up marriage to be a celibate. They are both beautiful callings, but I could see some difficulty with either choice. It helps to know that life is hard as it is anyway. Celibacy is a good thing but I would have to exclude another great thing in life, namely marriage and the possibility of a family altogether. On the flip side it had many benefits. On one hand celibacy would leave more time for prayer, and personal cultivation. On the other hand marriage would be nice. They both require generosity with time and service. I have seen that go wrong at home, so I knew that could be a difficult choice to live with. I was worried about all the normal things that people always stress about, what will my spouse be like, what type of job would I have, where would we live, what kind of parent will I be? All of these things would percolate in my mind, but this one thing seemed a great dilemma for me. In either case my mom was a lesbian. A million other things could be said about why I should choose one route over the other, but my mom's homosexuality was the biggest obstacle, in my own mind. It seems shallow, but there is an explanation.

It seemed like the road ahead of me forked between celibacy and marriage, and either of these could fulfill my life's journey, but the common obstacle was this one subject. I had tried to bury it in the past but it was always there. I tried avoiding it but it seemed that I would have to start acknowledging publicly that my mom is gay. No... I couldn't! My big dilemma was, what would it be like to be a priest who has an actively gay mom? What would people think of me? Would they treat me differently? If I got married, I was picturing a solid Christian woman, who perhaps has the same religious affinity that my grandparents possessed. I pictured a woman from a good family. In my mind the best case scenario would be that my wife would accept me and marry me, and she may accept my mother, but it would be shaky. Her family on the other hand might reject my mom, and they wouldn't have anything to do with me either. Notice that I was so worried about myself, me, me, me. I had some maturing to do. I was selfish, but certainly it was a real problem for me. Mom's homosexuality had affected my past so much, but I was fearsome that it would permeate my future life just as negatively as it had before in my past. I finally wanted to be honest about my life. However, what if rather than lying, telling the truth could cost me a lot? I was a young guy and there was much weighing on my mind.

I couldn't have it all figured out, I was only nineteen years old at this point. Many of us, millennials, are stressed because we don't exactly know what we want to do with ourselves after high school. We have so many questions, and some may have similar complexities to their questions like I had. A bit of a rush is good when making choices because our time is limited, but we shouldn't worry about what our lives will be like in five years. Five years from now doesn't exist. I was only going to meet the director of vocations, and nothing was set in stone.

Later on, when I got to know him, I realized that he was a holy man and he became a person that I hold in high regard. He was always very encouraging. I just had to take the next step. I was to only be concerned with the first step, and not preoccupied with steps number twelve or forty-seven. It was simple really. I met with the priest at my grandparents' home and we spoke about the possibility of priesthood for my life. We discussed it in some depth and he was very willing to answer any questions that I had. I mainly had logistical questions such as: where would I be going for seminary, how would I get there, how to apply to the diocese and the seminary itself, and I even ventured to ask if I could still have a girlfriend while being there? He answered all of my questions, but of course the answer to the last one was a resounding no. I wasn't crushed, I kinda knew the answer but I had to be sure. He gave me some information on the Roman Catholic priesthood and I kept learning about it.

I was a little nervous but I was warming up to the idea of exploring the priesthood. I think that today, we millennials, are presented with far too many options at times and we don't know what to do with them. Sometimes we are also told that we have time to figure things out, and certainly we do but the time isn't limitless. Not to add pressure, but our time is short so we can't afford to be listless. We have to tend towards some goal. It is good to be in the moment. The perfect antidote to listlessness is balance and discipline. We must be in the present knowing that it is shaping the future. Easier said than done.

I did my best to keep this in mind. I began the application process. It was more thorough than I could have imagined. I had to write a mini-biography first. I had to do a battery of tests with a psychologist, then I did several fill in the bubble scantron questionnaires. They requested that I provide a description of what I saw when viewing a series of Rorschach ink blots, and I also did a memory test. I was also asked similar questions from both the director of vocations and the psychologist. They asked things such as if I liked women, whether I was gay or not, they asked also if I was suicidal? They asked what type of girls had I dated. The psychologist asked if I was a virgin and I was honest with everything. That was important. It was difficult to be honest about my past, but it was a crucial step.

I was accepted and I was eager to begin this new journey. The thought of priesthood was sincerely on my heart and I had to address it. I wanted to know that I had given it a true shot and that I had thoroughly addressed it. I also wanted to avoid a midlife crisis, to avoid waking up at age forty only to come to the realization that the priesthood maybe was for me. I can't be faulted for being sincere. I was finally beginning to be more of a sincere person and simply honest with myself. I received an acceptance letter from the bishop and I knew that this would be arduous, but what real adventure isn't arduous?

I will jump a little in the future to my days in the seminary. These next words encouraged me during my formation at seminary. A cousin of mine, for the sake of anonymity we will refer to him as the Shatmaster, wrote me a neat and inspiring postcard while I was there. It was crude, humorous, and enlightening all at once. He said the following to me:

"Dear Daniel,
I remember my first day in Cali. San Francisco was still this mysterious ball of life full of beauty and dirt. My very first class, of my very first day, my very first college moment! We went around the room, calling out our names and speaking a little something about ourselves. I was a few years older than most of the pups around me, I said, 'my name is Shatmazter, I'm currently homeless and I'm fuckin excited to be here.' My professor David Choon Lee (Vietnamese) responded 'Rad'. David turned out to be my favorite teacher ever, and he meant what he said. Not, 'yeah you're homeless, good luck with that shit' - but 'sweet, you sacrificed something to be here, you're in the moment'.

And I think that is what it's all about, the risk and no chance of failure, no possibility of success. "Sitting at home masturbating, cruising the internet, eating hot pockets, sure you may be satisfying the moment but you're sacrificing nothing. Get into a gallery, publish yourself, knock goals down one at a time, and you'll find the domino effect in no time,' is what he told us. I'm super excited for you Dan, ever since you popped out of the womb you've been on a quest for knowledge, ravenous for the facts. I remember sitting on grandma and grandpa's couch in Pinetop, I'm reading Edward O. Wilson, my favorite scientist, I glance over and there's Daniel, sitting next to me with one of my books. You were so young and hairy it was comical, the book was upside down, and it was nearly midnight. You were so not old enough to read! But that didn't stop you from looking, from probing the pages, from searching. And now you're kicking ass at a dope college. You're right where you should be. Attack the day, apply the shit out of yourself. Sacrifice!
BONZAI DANIEL-SAN! BONZAIII!"

I was sure that I wanted to attend seminary. My home parish had a going away party for me. I was lavished with encouraging words, cake, and gift-cards. Many people were supportive of me. It made sense to many people in my family and to others in town that I would go to seminary. My grandparents were pillars in our community as far as people of faith. I was involved in my parish. I wasn't a golden child by any extension of the word, but I was prone to the sacred and religious. As a child I used to 'play Mass' and I tried to get my other cousins to play with me, but they were never enthused about it. I didn't understand why they weren't interested. Reluctant, they would join. I had one of them be the cross bearer (we used a broom), and two of them were candle bearers. I had few friends so that divine spark was always a bit more pronounced in me than it was in others. I was preparing myself mentally to go to seminary. My mother was very encouraging. She was eventually convinced that I would become a priest. Grandpa was sure that I would complete my studies and that I would one day be ordained a priest. It was warm, this feeling. I was embarking on a journey to be a part of something greater than myself. It was beyond me in many ways.

My mother was on board with me going to seminary. We had been pretty sure that I had moved to Argentina with the intention of staying so as a consequence, that goodbye was more painful. There was an urgency in the air when I parted for Argentina. This one was much different. My mother and I planned a trip to Columbus, Ohio, where the seminary was located. It was our first flight together to a different state. We touched down and we got a rental vehicle. I saw a couple of Tim Horton's coffee shops, a Hardies, and a Big Boy restaurant. The highways were a bit beat up and they weren't as ample as the ones in Arizona. We were finally pulling up to the seminary. The architecture was amazing, it was like a little piece of Europe right here in the U.S. We moved my things into my dorm room. We made a trip to a nearby Target to gather some final things to get my room ready. Once we arrived back to the seminary I met my future formation adviser who would help me journey in seminary. He seemed genuinely nice and full of life. It was a stark contrast to most priests that I had met from back home, as far as age and the energy they exuded. Some were old and looked like death. This priest had his expectations of me, and he had read my autobiography so he was very understanding. I never experienced a moment with him in which he wasn't supportive. He was always a positive role-model, and this was something I had never experienced from another man before. It was a nice change of pace. He showed us the chapel and my mother and I prayed there. I thanked God that I was finally getting the college experience I wanted, to live in a dorm and someplace else that wasn't home, all of those type of things. It was neat to bond with my mother during this time. Mom then had to leave for home and I was going to be living in Columbus for the academic year, very possibly for the next four years of my life. It was an amazing support to have my mother come and drop me off, it meant the world to me.

Mom returned to Arizona and I was on a quest now. When you first arrive to seminary the expectation that you will typically have of yourself, is that you will definitely become a priest. I wanted to discover my calling but that entails beginning an existential quest. I began this journey and I made friends fairly quickly. I met my roommate, Andy. He is a great guy from Indiana. He is intelligent, hardworking, dependable, humble, and best of all, simply fun to be around. He and I clicked immediately. I still keep in touch with another guy from Indiana, Johnny. He is a very diligent and studious guy, but he is down to earth. Johnny is also gifted with music. He is one of my best friends even to today. We have some funny drunk nights spent in good conversation and laughter. We would spend some nights studying and we would sometimes decide to get some grub at three in the morning. We were both nigh-owls so we were always up very late. Some of our funniest and meaningful conversations happened during that time. Those memories are forever seared into my mind. There was also a Polish-American priest there as well. He was from New Jersey. He was tall and some people found him to be imposing and intimidating. I was used to my grandfather's strict discipline, so that was a non-issue for me. We did have some friction but this man, this priest of God, genuinely cared for me. He once told me that I have a heart like John Paul II's. He tried to be uplifting towards me and he was. Shortly thereafter, the next day, a little Guatemalan-American guy came and knocked on my door. He had seen me previously and he decided that he would come and introduce himself. He let me know that his name is Martin. He and I talked a little bit and he told me that he had a twin. I met his twin, Pedro, the next day. They were from Alabama and I quickly connected with these guys. Martin later left the seminary and Pedro remained for four years. Pedro and I later developed a good friendship. We hold each other accountable and we help one another grow. One great thing about being in a national seminary is that you can become widely connected if you are open to others. In addition to that I became friends with people, who outside of the seminary context, I probably wouldn't have considered establishing a friendship with. None of this was coincidence, there is a reason behind everything in life.

The first year I was just in love with my life in seminary. It was like a yearlong retreat. During that time I learned a little bit about philosophy, and basic education. I learned much about the beauty of the church and it's universality, the uniformity of its message across the nation and the world. My knowledge of the church grew. Once during the academic year they had a speaker come and demonstrate how to conduct oneself with proper etiquette. My second year there we had psychologist come and speak to us about how to be celibate and still maintain a healthy sexuality. She touched on topics such as appropriate boundaries, healthy and non-enmeshed relationships, good habit forming, and healthy outlets. She also gave us funny scenarios that were meant to teach us how to be open to others while keeping appropriate boundaries. In the scenarios we had to deal with Flirty Fionas, Clingy Cassandras, Bossy Bills, as well as the awkward guy who never understands social cues. It was quite humorous to say the least. She was a fun guest speaker and incredibly insightful. We had plenty of healthy outlets at seminary and I had stability, something I didn't have during my earlier years. We had tons of books to read, board games, and the best of it all, was the fraternity we shared.

I also began to realize how flawed it can be, because the church is constituted of men and women. Before seminary, I viewed it as a vast worldwide organization that was divine, I viewed it as an institution placed here directly by God. I think many of the upperclassmen got carried away with the latter notion. Some men were just full of themselves. Instead of being a bridge to Christ they probably served more as an obstacle. I digress, I guess we all can be that way sometimes. Some Catholics can tend to focus on the rules way too much, and this can undermine the mission they have set out to accomplish. I don't ignore the rules on social teaching or worship but when emphasized too much, the legality easily becomes legalism. It was regimented and it becomes easy to equate the following of a rule with being holy. We shouldn't ignore rules certainly not, but if we forget to love God and our fellow man, then we are doing a pointless exercise.

It was all a developmental process. I was constantly learning. I had several ups and downs as should be expected. It was a combination of several things that deterred me from the idea of becoming a priest. The principal one is that by the end that first year my desire to become a priest had diminished. That sentiment would solidify during the summer where I was assigned to live at a parish with a couple of priests. Initially it was my attempt to warm up to the idea of celibacy and living a life of solitude. Some people live this life and are joyful and fulfilled. Other negative influences were how some of the upperclassmen were rigid guys that hardly smiled. They, along with a couple of the priests, lacked a deep spirituality. Most followed the rules exactly and that became a point of pride for them. I could clearly see there was a contrast between the theology they were learning, and the practical application of it in life. Yes we recited prayers and went to Mass daily but all of that should have permeated every aspect of our lives. I think I easily could slip into a similar attitude. I do like to learn from other people's mistakes, not to be judgmental, but in order to avoid those same errors.

Conversely, several guys should not have been admitted to the seminary. Some men that were admitted to the seminary were not psychologically sound. I could only guess what their background is. From the outset I was hoping to be a priest, but increasingly more and more I was also hesitant to continue being a seminarian for my diocese. The diocese had also filed for bankruptcy due to settling sexual abuse allegations against clergymen. I don't know the widespread damage and pain this caused for the victims and survivors most especially, but it was difficult for me to stomach. I didn't understand why clergymen and even bishops, not just in my diocese, had allowed this to occur. How could you comprehend why several leaders turned a blind eye to this, how they could do this to their own flock or to the world. Geoffrey Chaucer spoke of similar disparity between the clergy and the faithful and corruption during his modern day using the following analogy, "if the gold should rust, what of the silver? - if the shepherds are lost, then what of the sheep?" Once the news began to dawn on us in our diocese, I began to urge my reconsideration of seminary and the priesthood altogether. I prayed about it earnestly and I began to accept the idea of leaving the seminary as the first year began to conclude. I am generally good at transitions because of moving around all of the time. I had a lot of time for reflection in seminary and this helped me put things a little more in perspective.

I would look back on my year and really exam it. I made good friends and though I struggled academically I had much support from the priests and faculty to make it through. I was grateful for all of this in my life but I knew that this would only be temporary and the path I was looking towards something that was permanent. I didn't feel at home in my diocese. I witnessed some other seminarians from other diocese who had great relationships with their bishops. My good friends from Alabama had their bishop and priests visiting them all of the time. I never received that except once. There was a seminarian from my same diocese at the same seminary, but he and I weren't friends. I believe most friendships are spontaneous, but I didn't have that with any of the priests or seminarians from my diocese. I was always a lone wolf since childhood. Maybe God wants for me to be a lone wolf, but admittedly sometimes it flat-out sucks. I was making genuine friendships and I knew that seminary wasn't forever, but even then it became increasingly more difficult to envision myself as a priest. I didn't have all the answers about my place in this world. I obviously believe that we are meant for heaven, but I didn't know how I was going to specifically accomplish that. I didn't have all of the answers then and I still don't.

I was conflicted while at seminary. It is my impression that in Catholicism in general, priests are placed on a pedestal. Being so deep and close to the church I came to realize it. I remember going back to my diocese for the Chrism Mass and for Easter break. The Mass at the cathedral had so many people, the temple was packed. At times people lose focus on their faith and focus more on different religious figures. I thought the Mass itself was beautiful and many people there were pious, but sometimes the depth of Catholicism is lost and overlooked. Some priests are treated like kings in other countries and that's no exaggeration. If a priest can correctly be humble then that's good, he doesn't leave room for any of that. If a priest basks in that, he is delusional. It is always a beautiful thing to witness a priest who is truly dedicated to God and his people. I think the world also admires this, but it could never produce this. Some people can use this for good ends and others for an ill purpose. It can be a power that some hold to become saintly and to help others to do the same, and still others become treacherous while simply turning people off.

I saw many of my own inadequacies as well and I figured out that I was not called to be a priest for a diocese. I began to look into different orders and groups within the church, and I also began to contact their vocations directors as well. Shortly before the conclusion of my first year at seminary I began to entertain the idea of visiting Turkey. I planned a trip there for the summer which was fast approaching. Turkey is a country that you can try to imagine but you will always fall short, and realize it once you have visited. It was time to conclude my first year of seminary. I was grateful to have that first year but I was leaning towards not coming back. I did know however, that I would take my trip to Turkey. Afterwards I would see my summer internship through at a parish in my diocese. I was eager to see what I would for sure decide on. I was most eager to take the next step. I decided that much.

I went home for a couple of days to be with my family. That time was brief and it was peaceful to spend it with my grandparents and my mom. Soon I had to leave. Much like Argentina, I had learned much about the land before visiting, but I would discover a whole new world in Turkey. In discovering new places, it forces me to take a honest look at myself. It forces some soul searching. Change of place doesn't mean change of heart but it brings new perspectives. I arrived in Istanbul and it was like New York City, fast paced and people don't stop to consider you. I contacted my friend in Northern Turkey in the city of Edirne. I saw much of the countryside on my way over by train. It was then that I realized that in the city people are constantly on the rush to someplace else, and it seems like they never arrive to their destination. Unlike many of the citizens this was a learning experience for me so I wasn't rushing. I was taking everything in. I needed to focus on my own life and I was doing that. I enjoyed the silent retreats at seminary, but I often find that a healthy way for me to be alone is abroad. It helps me put my life into perspective.

I arrived to Edirne on the border of Greece and Bulgaria. I travelled all day long, and night had fallen by the time I arrived. My friend met me and took me to a hotel run by the government, it was old. I spent the night. When I woke up the next morning it hit me, "I am in Turkey! I will get to explore this country and learn the language for the next month." I had studied the language for years since being a teenager and I was constantly speaking to Turks back in Arizona, now I am finally here." Visiting Turkey definitely brought me closer to my faith and it also helped indirectly to reconcile with my mother. Remember change of place doesn't mean change of heart, but this was a new scene for me. People who have a different way of life can have a great impact on how we perceive ourselves and the world.

My perspective was broadened on life. Never before this trip and up to this point had I been so immersed in Islam. It was so tangible. I visited an ancient mosque in Edirne. I had done some homework on Turkey but I would only learn more about it the longer I would spend there, for instance I didn't know that Muslims ritualistically purify certain parts of their bodies, such as their hands up to the elbows their head and feet before reading from the Quran. It was also neat to see how deeply rooted the citizens' identity was in their country, and as a result they tend to be an unapologetic people. I felt that I fit in while my stay in Turkey.

Several things helped me feel welcomed. The people there were extremely hospitable. The delicacies were amazing, nothing quite comforts us like food. I tried many traditional Turkish dishes whether home cooked or in different restaurants. Turkey is an extremely ethnically diverse country, but the citizens are proud to call themselves a Turk. The entire experience was as rich as the food. For instance, one night I was taking a boat similar to a ferry from Izmit across a section of the Sea of Marmara. I was supposed to catch a bus later, which was on the other side towards Istanbul. It was a cool night on the water. The water was choppy and I could clearly tell that I was on a boat, the movement of the deck underneath my feet made sure of that. People were up and about and speaking to one another. It was neat to see all of their interactions and they were all citizens, and I was a foreigner along for the ride. The fog enveloped us briefly for a moment so the captain sounded the horn to warn any other vessels. I was mesmerized, this was life in Turkey. I eventually sat down, mainly to retain my balance, when I looked up and noticed how the stars beautifully illumined the otherwise dark evening. The sea cast a beautiful reflection of the moon that rose from underneath. I was eager to see what Istanbul was all about, but I also was pondering my life. I pondered whether I should return to seminary or what I should do with my life. I had many answers and solutions but they didn't outnumber my questions. I got off once we stopped, I eager for the future.

The best way for me to prepare for the future, was to soak in the moment. I was captivated. Istanbul is so beautiful. The name is a Greek derivative and it simply means 'the city.' It was quite the city. I visited the former Byzantium temple, Hagia Sophia present there today, a remnant of the former civilization and city when it was formerly known as Constantinople. It was later converted into a mosque, but it is presently a museum. The architecture is immaculate and I cannot do it justice in words, but Christianity should always be this tangible. This temple makes all mega churches in America pale in comparison. Of course I do not argue that it is not a question of faith, that is what matters most. Though I can say that due to the beauty of the culture there, it is easier to live and share the faith. 'The city' was deeply permeated and defined by several cultural identities and it was wondrous to see. I am not sure that this can be experienced in the United States to this same degree, but it makes you desire to grow in faith. I also felt similar in other cities. The family I stayed with was truly devout, and that is something that rubs off onto other people. Even though the family was Muslim I was beginning to think about the priesthood once again. It was a refreshing perspective to faith and there was a simplicity that they possessed. There is a quote from Pope Benedict XVI that I think deeply resonates with this train of thought, "Human beings are relational, and they possess their lives, themselves, only by way of relationship. I alone am not truly myself, but only in 'you' and with 'you' am 'I' myself. To be truly a human being means to be related in love, to be 'of' and 'for'." I was becoming more open to discover how people think and what people believe. I was understanding other individuals, cultures, and societies, it is a must in life to understand. It is a must to be understanding. Very few people today have a historical memory. The reason that this is a detriment is because everybody's got a story to tell. It helped to be in a foreign country because I had to deal with myself. It can be scary but it is necessary and I was willing. Once self-discovering begins we can soon begin to understand others. It is also in discovering other people that we learn more about ourselves as well.

One of the other cities that I was able to visit was Antioch. I was deeply impacted there. When I arrived the faith there was palpable. I would see mosques, synagogues, and churches all built next to each other. Imams, Arabs, Alevis, and priests trickled into the city, making it an elaborate tapestry. They each came from their respective squares. There aren't enough words, the culture and faith found there is simply tangible and alive. I went to a site of ancient ruins. This visit solidified my confidence in Christianity because so many people before me had lived here and shared my same faith. It can be proved factually that Mary and John the Evangelist lived in Ephesus, another great city of antiquity. I was able to see, smell, touch, and learn from antiquity itself. It was just amazing beauty injected into my life and it was therapeutic.

My outlook changed in an immediate sense. I came to greatly appreciate the United States and its relative stability. In discovering other countries and societies, you also discover what home is like and how it is similar or different to these different places. Turkey has two main spheres of influence, the Eastern side and the Western side. While I was in Turkey there was some turmoil among some people there. Towards the end of my stay there were the Gezi Park protests. I was on the Anatolian side and I was unable to access the European side. The government blocked access to Facebook and Twitter, and it was not logistically practical to call my mother for a few days. It became a little unsafe. Many people were protesting and rioting in the streets. In retrospect, Turkey changed my long-term perspective on life because it has given me a hunger and thirst to meet new people, to travel abroad. New cultures can teach us new ways to view the world, they can cause an interior commotion or an interior peace, new ways to be understanding, and new ways to live. Even if we have differences with them, they can teach us more about ourselves and where we stand in life. This doesn't mean we must accept everything, we can't be people pleasers either. However, we must accept the things that we cannot change such as our past. It is gone, so let's learn from our past. I had gained a new perspective, and I was to arrive home for a few days before beginning my summer assignment in my diocese. It made me appreciate family, and I particularly liked their cohesiveness. People in Turkey tend to be very family oriented, they are always there for one another. We have hardships that come our way, but laughter is a perfect antidote to all of this. That was the biggest take away from my trip in Turkey, and now I was going home.

Once I arrived to Arizona I would have more than a couple of days to get ready for my parish internship in Show-Low, Arizona. I unpacked, washed, and repacked everything that I needed. All the meanwhile I was still trying to process my trip to Turkey, to really let it sink in. An excellent place to continue to process my trip was my grandparents' home, being that my grandparents have a very strong cultural and religious identity. They hoped the best for me during my assignment, and I did also. My mother was more encouraging to me than ever before so it helped me take the assignment on with the best attitude and with the most sincerity. I would have to have a real look at myself and I hoped that it would confirm a lot for me. Just like that night on the boat in Turkey, I knew I was going to have to really take in the experience and examine myself.

When you are doing anything for the first time, other people can tell you what their own impression was of an event or an activity but they can never really do it justice. An experience must be your own to fully appreciate it. I couldn't have many expectations, whether good or bad, because they would be banished most likely on my assignment. I was just trying to be open to what the experience would hold for me and this seemed the best attitude for me to have. I arrived in Show-Low with the hope of finding an answer to either continue or to withdraw from seminary formation. Father Mark was the pastor of the parish. He assumed a sort of laissez-faire attitude which was great for me because I was becoming more and more independent. The other priest that I had the opportunity to work and engage in ministry with, was an Indian priest who was new to the United States. His name is Father Gummadi. We visited sick people and he would hear my confession at times. He helped me grow much but it was mutual. I introduced him to various fast food restaurants such as Wendy's, McDonald's, and Burger King. He particularly enjoyed the Baconator and a chocolate frosty, but who doesn't? We also had Denny's and I will just say that was quite the experience. Father Gummadi didn't know how to drive and I took a chance and I began to teach him how to drive. He almost wrecked the parish car and I got visibly frustrated with him. It was an experience to grow nonetheless. Father Gummadi was the best part of my assignment.

I was also able to visit the doctor who helped deliver me. He didn't know who I was obviously, but it was neat to see that. He gave my mother encouraging words during my delivery, "Do not be afraid of having a kid." He was a good man. Serving Mass for the Mexican population there was nothing short of touching. I hung out with them a lot. We would frequently hang out, they would have me over for dinner, or we would catch a movie. I noted that they are people of tremendous faith and they were genuinely interested in my journey. They wanted to know what I studied and were curious to see what the future held for me. I answered their questions but wasn't certain about my future yet, despite the rich experiences of the summer there. I had a couple of rough patches during the my stay in Show-Low as well. The main struggle for me was celibacy. I kept my celibacy and chastity during this entire summer and that was good for me. I enjoyed my summer experience, but I couldn't imagine myself living my entire life in solitude. I did enjoy solitude at some times but not for extended periods. Being abroad helps stimulate my thoughts and it helps me truly discover myself, but I couldn't picture myself immersed in the celibate lifestyle. I am getting back to the Pope Benedict quote from earlier, we need good relationships to be able to truly be ourselves. Sometimes our different relationships can be rough but aren't those opportunities for each of us to grow, for each of us to be understanding and loving? Of course celibate priests can be fulfilled people even though they themselves do not marry. They may not have wives and children but they have friends, mothers and fathers, and many spiritual brothers and sisters that they help guide and are guided by as well. They also serve other people, many times they visit the sick and elderly that nobody else would visit otherwise. They certainly have the time on their hands and availability to do so. I learned this in seminary and on my assignment, though it is a great lifestyle, I also had to be honest with myself and recognize that it wasn't for me. This perspective was the main one that helped me grow still closer to my grandparents and my mother as well. We had become estranged from each other because of both of our attitude towards one another. Growing closer to my mother was and is as simple as saying it. It requires sacrifice, it requires looking past our differences and meeting each other where we are at, it requires that we simply consider one another. It is a simple principle, 'you get out of life what you put into it', but damn isn't it tough! It cannot be tougher than making life more complicated than it already is, can it?

I had concluded that I would not continue in seminary by the end of my summer assignment but my family was very hopeful that I would see it through, particularly my grandparents, and more specifically my grandfather. I could break the news to them but I also didn't want to disappoint my grandmother nor my grandfather. This was a dream for them that I was going to become a priest. It wasn't my dream. I didn't have my dream all figured out. I missed my dream of having the family that I wanted as a child, but I will not get that time back. That didn't mean I couldn't focus on the present. I could definitely work at becoming closer to my mother and I could have my own family one day, that was my hope. I mentioned the possibility of leaving seminary to my grandparents and my mother. My grandmother wanted me to continue and get my degree. In my mind I didn't want a liberal arts degree if it wasn't something that I wasn't passionate about, and it is pretty useless as far as getting a job. My grandfather was in love with the idea of me becoming a priest. My mother was the most understanding, she wanted me to do the right thing, and for the right thing to make me happy. Mom wanted me to live a good life and that was it. It was comforting to know that she hoped the best for me.

I decided that I needed to give seminary another shot. I returned for my second year of undergraduate seminary formation. It was definitely helpful to be consistent. It was rough, to say the least. My heart wasn't in it but I was at seminary, so I made the most of it. I was back in touch with my good friends there. The newness had worn off by then and it was a struggle to stay completely focused with it. It is a curious thing to be in one place wishing to be in another, and that is with many things in life. My academic struggles persisted but I found much encouragement from my professors and the priest who were guiding us in our formation. I met with tutors and I made use of the library and writing center to improve my skills and the quality of my papers. It was overbearing at times, I wasn't so much interested in studying philosophy as I was invested in discovering my path. I hadn't discovered my path yet, but I was increasingly convinced that it wasn't the priesthood. I communicated this to my formation advisor. It was helpful that we had this support there to help us make good decisions. At the end of the day, I must go to bed at peace with myself and with God.

I had some understanding friends to bounce my ideas off of, and also some time in silence and prayer to examine myself. I was able to really collect myself and gather my thoughts. I think that this time I spent in solitude was useful to me because it also allowed me to be with myself. I was able to look at my past self. I thought about the future and what it could hold for me, but I didn't want to dwell on it very much. I also thought of my assignment from the summer that had just passed. There were several times through those brief two months that people would come to the parish looking for help. Some needed financial help, some needed some words of wisdom, others needed a word of encouragement and the priest was there to help them. I witnessed a lot it and I realized that many of them were looking for the same thing. Some only needed attention, some needed to be understood. Some were victims and others made themselves the victims but in any case, they needed to be reached out to. Some made decisions that brought them to rock bottom and others didn't have much of a choice in what life threw their way.

These people that came and visited the parish decided to reach out and the priest didn't turn them away. Some were rape victims, some were victims of domestic violence from their spouse, some of the women had a recent abortion and they didn't know how to process it, so they looked for guidance. Others felt trapped and with no place else to go. It made me remember my mother and how rough it was growing up with her. That is when it became most evident to me, during that summer that I shouldn't ostracize my mom because of our differences but I should accept her for who she is. Some of our differences in ideologies may never be reconciled, but that doesn't mean we cannot be reconciled as a people. It was also a big help that I was reading Scripture and waking up in the morning to go to Mass. I prayed more in seminary and that distance from my family helped me see a bigger picture. Sometimes we miss the forest because we are standing to close to the trees, and seminary gave me a unique perspective. I also learned this from traveling abroad and from my friends from seminary, who represented several places from around the country. No one grows in a vacuum. A seed needs water, minerals, light, warmth, and nutrition to grow. I was finally getting these wholesome relationships. They compelled me to sit down and listen to other people in honest conversations. It taught me to be a better listener and to speak less in conversation. It required that I step out of myself for a little to understand myself. I needed some time away to peel back some layers and really look at myself. I had the thought of religious life on my mind for a while and I wanted to look into that. It was a quest that would take me out of my comfort zone. This was a question that would take me far away from what I was familiar with.

I wanted to let my mind roam freely for a little, and I coupled this with a trip to a remote region in Central America. After my Christmas break I decided that I would take a trip down to Guatemala to look into a religious order called the Maryknoll missionaries. I was still exploring the possibility of joining a religious group, a lingering curiosity left over from the summer. The timing of the trip was something that I considered very carefully.

I decided the winter would be the best time for me to view this place, due to the tropical temperatures that blanket the area all year round. Guatemala City is beautiful city and some of the colonial influences can still be seen today. It is a city surrounded by the jungle in every direction. As I was flying in I was enraptured by the beauty of the mountainous terrain and sea of green trees which wrapped around this gem. The baroque churches were some of the more prominent types of architecture that I noticed there, alongside the old colonial style government buildings. I enjoyed the city briefly for a day, and I toured a museum but I wasn't really going to be sightseeing. I was supposed to be on mission and on a spiritual retreat. I got in touch with the group that I would be staying with. The Maryknoll missionaries are a neat group, one of their gifts is to live alongside indigenous and native peoples in remote regions in the world to spread the Gospel. Many of them learn the indigenous languages and dialects in order to be better servants. I spent two weeks with them and it was one of the most humbling experiences. The citizens in the aldea (county) of K'iche' is a beautiful area. People there are simple and sometimes shy. I spent time there in prayer and in service to others, but they don't finish a day of missioning to only retreat into their commodities and privileged lives, no they become poor with the people.

Here is an example to illustrate the lifestyle of austerity that these men would assume. We ate whatever the locals offered us. It didn't matter how little or how simple the food was that they offered, we accepted it with gratitude. One morning I was having breakfast, and it consisted of a small bowl of black beans, eggs, and a miniature cut of beef in the middle. The priest told me to eat up my food and to eat as many corn tortillas because I wouldn't know when I would be eating again. I ate, to have strength for a possibly long day ahead of us. It was liberating though, to serve others and to not worry about the more superficial things in life. I felt very alive in Guatemala.

We spent some time in this aldea and we even went as far as traveling up to the Pèten, Guatemala. It was paradise. It is the site of the enormous Mayan Biosphere Reserve. The mornings there are nothing short of majestic. When I would wake up in these Northern mountains it was crazy to witness how the soft blanket of mist and fog would settle on the unending sea of jungle. The sunlight would hit my face, and I wasn't greeted by the crowing of a rooster, but rather an entire jungle would come to life and I would wake up to all of the different sounds. I could hear exotic birds, the different apes calling out, along with many other wild animals. The wind would brush strongly against the trees and I would get up ready to start another day of prayer and hard work.

After prayer and breakfast we would visit many people in some of the remotest towns and villages. The most touching experience that I had there was to visit the children in a small poor community. The kids there lived in a landfill and they heard us arrive. We had food, candy, and basic toiletries and necessities for them. As soon as they heard us they immediately came up to us. They were hungry and in desperate need of attention. They accepted the brother's generosity. I played games with them and they were always happy and joyful. It is amazing to see that children have all the same characteristics anywhere in the world. They have a simplicity that, unfortunately we as adults don't often possess. This unique experience inspired a strong desire in me to have children. After the day was over I would reflect on this, and also the direction that I was heading in life. I was going to return to seminary, but I was still struggling with the thought of becoming a priest. I couldn't envision it. I also didn't think that I could be a religious brother, the desire to have a family was too strong for me. I realized that I had been blessed with so much in life that I knew that I had to make something of myself. Once my experience was over, I flew back to Ohio to resume my studies there for my spring semester.

It was January 2014 and the seminarians were preparing to go and visit Washington D.C. for the annual March for Life demonstration. At this point my mom and I had already begun to open up to each other more about our past, and how things had unfolded from there. I had shared with her my experience from the previous year of the march. When speaking on the phone my mother and I would share about our how we viewed our past in our own eyes.

We spoke freely, without any reservations. She never realized the pain and loneliness I was going through, that feeling that can't really be captured in words. She shared with me her childhood and what that was like, but she also touched on what she was experiencing as I was growing up. It is obvious that we never really knew each other. I felt like I was meeting a new person. I also was beginning to understand her more. The honesty was so refreshing, and so necessary. Since we were being honest and I had spoken about the March for Life movement, my mother decided that she needed to reveal to me something from her past that came as a complete shock to me. My mother confessed to me that she previously had an abortion after I was born. I was shocked to hear her tell her story. My initial thought was that my mom had an abortion, how? It was a decision that had set the dynamic of pain and isolation for us. My initial thought was to think and maybe say something reactionary. The initial shock made me speechless at first. I paused enough for her to pick her story up again after a suspenseful silence.

Mom broke the silence, it was momentous. Mother told me that she was scared, she didn't have the means to support another child. I include myself in this, some would state the obvious and say that she shouldn't have gotten pregnant in the first place. Of course she shouldn't have, but she did and that was reality! She had an abortion, that was reality. It never helps to lodge those hypothetical 'should haves' and 'shouldn't haves' to people when they are opening up about something so difficult and hurtful. The more I listened to her the more I realized how alone she felt to be driven into a man's arms, to feel accepted. Furthermore, I realized that she felt out of options about raising another child when she didn't really have the means to do so, she didn't even have the means to bring the pregnancy to full-term. She also didn't want to disappoint her parents. An acquaintance of hers at the time presented her with the option of getting an abortion. My mother was desperate and I understand her. I could do nothing but listen to her. I don't condemn her, why add fuel to the fire? I am glad that I wasn't reactionary when I listened to her share something that she was so deeply hurt by. I now know that my mom felt as if she was stripped of her womanhood and true femininity. This explained so much to me, I even shed some tears, for the baby, but mostly for my mother. Slowly she has begun to heal and I have been along for her journey as well. It was a monumental step to share all of this with me, and it was then when we began to take those big steps towards reconciliation with each other. I think many people forgive in their hearts, but to reconcile is the real way to begin to fix those broken relationships. It was difficult at the beginning of this process, and it still is. Reconciliation takes a great effort but it is worth it. This new knowledge also forced me to examine myself deeply and to consider where I was heading. My mother and I were taking big steps to reconcile. I was also looking to reconcile with some hard truths.

Very few people knew about my mom's second pregnancy. As I am writing this only a handful of people know about this, my grandparents don't even know about this. If you are reading this, then it is no longer private information. It is no longer is private in the hope that other people can learn from these experiences. We make decisions, and the ripples cannot be contained like when we cast a stone into a still lake. Decisions are made. The ripples reverberate and we can't make them return. We can only watch the ripples. We can only listen and begin the dialogue that is necessary between people who love each other. We can begin to hear where they come from, what their motivations are. This is how we understand, because humans speak from the fullness of the heart.

I was growing closer to God in seminary, it was simply an easy environment to do that in. I was slowly learning to become more understanding. I had a lot of help. I was making very wholesome friendships, something that was still so new to me in life. Some guys in seminary considered everything about the human condition, and this helped foster in me a greater open-mindedness. The philosophy helped, but the prayer was perhaps the greatest help. It was this, and the hunger and willingness that Mom and I had to be heard and to hear the each other. It was the desire to know each other. I was growing closer to my mother. However, there was something that I had to come to terms with. I wasn't called to be a Catholic priest, I desired to discover whether I was called or not. I discovered a newfound love for my original dream, to have a family. Now I had discovered the truth about myself so I needed to move on. I knew the deep stirrings found in my heart when thinking about family life were there for a reason, and it was not merely a coincidence. My grandparents would be sad but I didn't really know what my grandfather would make of it. I was concerned about that but I was more preoccupied with being true to myself. I had to be honest with myself, for me and for no one else. It was difficult, but I had to make that step.

CHAPTER 7
KNOW THYSELF

Know thyself. Such a powerful and sometimes scary command for anyone. It is necessary to understand your own self to not grow stagnant in life. I began to discover myself in seminary. I was drawing closer to a decision that I had to make. I had to leave the place that was instrumental in discovering myself. I formally withdrew from priestly formation and I returned to Arizona. My mother initially thought that I left because of her lifestyle, and that I was ashamed of this fact. I had difficulty with her orientation, yes, but that was not cause for me to leave the seminary. I dispelled that notion. I made it clear to her that it was my independent choice to leave. I returned to Holbrook and I felt like a failure. I didn't want to be a part of that diocese, and I simply didn't want to be in seminary anymore. I was done with it. I felt like a failure because I didn't finish all of the formation to be had there, but I also knew that it wasn't for me. I had peace knowing that I wasn't called to be a catholic priest and I was now gearing myself to one day become a husband and a father. I had this intention deep in my heart, but I was going through a crisis because I didn't know what I was going to do as far as a career. I didn't know what I was going to do with my limited skill and knowledge.

My grandmother accepted me back home and was happy either way, but my grandfather was very disappointed and even angry with me. The transition was difficult. I had to live under my grandfather's rule again. He expected me to be quick at acting when doing chores. I constantly had various projects around the house to complete. I had to take short showers, and if I took too long he would switch the hot water off while I was still finishing up my business. I didn't think that leaving seminary entailed 'joining' the military. At least it seemed that way. We had arguments here and there. He expressed to me that he thought I used the church for my own benefit. I would argue that it simply wasn't true because seminary is a place for self-discovery, and I had discovered as much as knowing that I wasn't called to be a priest. My grandmother chimed in on my behalf. She recognized I didn't sign a dotted line the day I entered seminary. How could I know instantly, whether I was called or not? I was only nineteen years old when I entered. It was a process, and during this process I had come to a choice that took with my whole heart, and it was 'no' to the Roman Catholic priesthood.

Now I found myself back home and I had to continue my journey. I made my best effort to continue going to church when I first arrived. I was far from the strong faith-filled kid in Ahwatukee. I no longer had the stability and camaraderie that seminary could offer, but it mattered that I was being honest with myself and everyone else. I would accompany my grandparents to Mass every weekend. Then eventually I went to church on most weekends, and it was obvious to my grandfather. Slowly, I began to drift away from my faith. Infidelity starts with the little things. Eventually the tension between us culminated and Grandpa and I got into a heated argument. He kicked me out. I had to leave so that things could be smooth sailing for my grandparents and the tension would no longer be there. My grandmother cried. I packed my things and left for my mother's place. She and I spoke about everything that happened earlier during the day. I spent the night at her place, but I had to move on. I had to move on so I gathered my things, and I left for Phoenix to stay with a Catholic religious order called the Crosiers. I had community for about three months with them but I definitely felt alone. I felt that I failed my grandfather in all ways, that I couldn't live up to his expectations. This disappointment that I was feeling brought familiar notion about pleasing other people, and I felt like the lone wolf again. The lone wolf feeling only estranges you from the ones that matter in life. I began to despair, and it was easy to do because I was alone again. I grew angry towards God. My motto during this time was, "I hate God and God hates me." It was the attitude that I assumed and I began to live accordingly.

I did what I could to keep my mind occupied. I began to work at the airport and I made some friends there. I had a good friend, Melissa, that I met there. She is as much beautiful interiorly as she is beautiful exteriorly. What surprised me about her is that she was extremely down to earth. I made other friends at work and I began to go out a lot. I also had a few different attractive girlfriends during this time. Since my morals had gone out the window at this point I was becoming more independent from the church and from God as well. My thought during this time was that in the end no one really cares for you. I sincerely believed that no one gave a shit about me, and I accepted that. It was easy to slip into this mentality because at this point my life consisted of work during the week, and going out on the weekends. When only certain things in life can fulfill us, we find a million ways to remain empty. I didn't have fulfilling friendships, not nearby at least. I suppose you get what you put into life. Maybe I wasn't putting much into life but there was a void in me that I couldn't fill. There was a void where God belonged, where community belonged, and where my family belonged. Nothing else could fill it for me. I also struggled to know who I really was. I had learned about where I wasn't supposed to go in life, now I was preoccupied with finding where I was meant to go. Where am I headed? Why am I here, was the big question that I was thirsting to have answered. I was on an existential quest, and also in a crisis to search for meaning. I knew what brought me peace, but as young people, we easily try every other alternative. I had to search. I had to figure out who I was.

I was on this mental note when it occurred to me to take a backpacking vacation through Mexico. I was attempting to figure out my place in the world and it seemed a good way for me to surround myself with beauty. When I was in Turkey, the culture and religion touched me profoundly and I believed that true beauty and rich culture could always help keep me on track. I learned from philosophy and from the church that beauty is essential in life. Beauty evokes so many emotions at first, but on a deeper level it can help us get to the core of things in our hearts. I tried to remind myself of why I existed and what the beautiful things are in life. I was decisive, I wanted to take a trip to Mexico to learn more about myself and there was nothing to stop me. I was set, I went down to Mexico. I back-packed all over the entire country for three months. I saw Mexico City and on the outskirts, I saw the largest ancient Aztec city, Teotihuacan. The Nahuatl speaking Aztecs gave it this original name. It's meaning is fascinating, 'Where men become gods.' After some time, I arrived at the beach in Tulum in Quitana Roo. I spent a decent amount of time there. This is what is known as the Mayan Riviera. During the days the shallow water by the shore is extremely clear. It was fascinating to see much of the wildlife in the sea. Later that evening my Argentinian friend and I rolled up a joint and enjoyed it. It heightened my perception of everything around me. I was enjoying the feeling of the warm ocean touching my skin that night out at sea, and as I was floating I contemplated the sky. The massive moon beckoned me to search for meaning. Before this moment and since then, I have never experienced a clear sky so full of stars. I then began to deeply ponder what my life had been, up to that moment. I thought of where I was at, and where I was headed.

I remembered all of the people in my life that have been influential. I wondered how I could be whole. The still and quiet night invited me to be interiorly still and quiet. It was an invitation to stop in my journey to reflect on what it all had meant to me at that precise moment. I naturally thought of all my relationships. My relationship with my mom needed work and I knew that she felt the same way. Nature helped me get out of myself and to see things in a fuller way. I thought of all the craziness that I had gone through with my mom. It was that moment of peace and stillness that was instrumental in helping me face all of this. Slowly I began to recollect several of the more significant memories in my life. I remembered my sweetest moments in life. I also didn't shy away from the bitter ones. My mom had shared so much of her life with me that I had to take all that into account as well. I thought of how her background was something that also, directly and indirectly, touched my own life. It was also important to note how important I was becoming to her. Not all was lost. In fact, we were gaining ground in our relationship. It was with the accumulation of all of these thoughts that I was inspired to take some notes of what I was going through. Ever since Argentina I had written down some of the more significant experiences that helped build me up. I did the same in Turkey, and I have done it ever since. Then the lightbulb went off, and I got the initial idea to write this book. It would grant me the opportunity to use my hobby for the good of others. One way I knew I must write this book, was because I received the idea in a moment of peace. I had a desire to write about my journey which is always an ongoing one. I also had a desire to write about my mom's journey. There was something in our story that I felt we must share.

Many of the things that have happened to my mom and I have been trying, and even horrible. I would like to say that in discovering my mother's past I realized that I am not the only one who has suffered. To you reader, I would like to note that everyone has gone through some shit, and this isn't new news to you. No one is alone in this. It can be an act of God that we can continue in this life. It takes our effort, but sometimes it is just a gift, sometimes it is pure grace that we continue here. It can even be something as simple as one human acknowledging another. I had traveled a decent amount and I plan to travel some more during the rest of my life. Being around other people makes us come out of ourselves. So when we are uncomfortable around a lesbian mom, that drunk uncle, a pissed off boss, let's just acknowledge that we all have got some work to do. Don't be a doormat either, but keep this in the back of your mind. Before we can even begin to address another person's problem, we should really take a look at our own issues. The best example is the person who walks the walk. Some of us are more fortunate than others, in this same vein we should be understanding of others. Everyone has a battle to face, and my years of silence in loneliness will affirm that there is no way we can know what is in another person's heart. It is crazy how silence can bring us to a place of healing when for so many years it kept Mom and I frustrated and internally screaming. Silence is required in discussion in order to hear others. One mystic in the Orthodox church said something not so long ago that speaks to the same truth I am saying here. Father Seraphim Rose said, "Don't criticize or judge other people, regard everyone else as an angel, justify their mistakes and weaknesses, and condemn only yourself as the worst sinner. This is step one in any kind of spiritual life." He tells us to be humble. Essentially, we can't shout at the world to change if we haven't even examined ourselves in order to change.

Striking the balance between being independent and not having enmeshed relationships with family members is not always so easy to find, as with anything that requires balance. As my high was wearing off, I was also thinking about where I stood in life and what I needed to do to have a good relationship with God. That is a lifelong endeavor. In the past it was helpful to reflect on my experiences so I decided to do that. One of greater thoughts that came to mind was the feeling of loneliness, especially in relation to God. I know that I am not the only person who has been in a crowd and has still felt alone. I am not the only one who has been estranged from my family because of differing thoughts on moral questions and social norms.

I was back in Mexico and was just off the shore, still gazing at the stars. The night was similar to the one in Turkey. I thought about the brevity of life. I didn't have many fulfilling relationships in Phoenix, meanwhile my grandparents were getting older, and my mother and I still had some edges to smooth out in our relationship. I wanted to write about my life in the hopes that this could help people realize that reconciliation with loved ones is not impossible, though it sure as hell is difficult. It would still require much work on my part. I finished my trip in Mexico feeling rejuvenated. I returned to the states with a fresh perspective, but one that I had to apply to my life. I needed to be intentional. I was happy to see how this new direction in my life would unfold for me.

For my mother and I to grow closer together it would require much effort on both our behalves. We do not concede on our personal beliefs but this shouldn't be an obstacle to knowing one another. My mother brought me into the world that's a fact, but I didn't ask to be here. "She was going to have to take the first step"… if I would have continued with this attitude then maybe you wouldn't be reading this book, and just maybe my mom and I wouldn't be where we are today. The temptation to think this way always resurges, but we have to overcome it constantly. There is no magic trick, we just have to relinquish our ego. Forgiveness is talked about far too little nowadays. I think a lot of us are self-absorbed, conceited, and prideful and that is why forgiveness is rare to encounter. Everybody can forgive.

Furthermore, reconciliation is talked about less, and it takes honest conversation with our own selves and with others to achieve it. I had to grow in my relationship with my mom yes, but I also had to be independent. There were many things that I did not understand about relationships and how they're supposed to work, when I was a kid. The more I was able to grow and mature, and get deeper into self-discovery, the more I have also realized some things about the people surrounding me. It is because of my mom's co-dependency, that I had a difficult childhood, and it wasn't necessarily because my mother is a lesbian. Of course, it cannot be denied that my mom being a lesbian was more than difficult at some times. Whether she was with different men instead of women, her co-dependency would have affected me the same altogether. That hurt little girl inside of her was still looking to heal, she was looking to be loved and looking to mature. Her co-dependency made her paralyzed in life and her homosexuality blinded me to it. I discovered more of my mom when I could look past the fact that she is lesbian. I began to see my own-self in her. I could identify with her, maybe not to the exact same degree but there was progress in that. I was becoming more independent and it was healthy to examine myself. In doing this I came to a better understanding of who I am and who my mom is to me.

Along with this greater independence I was taking up greater responsibility for my actions and my life. I stopped playing the blame game and began to take responsibility for where I was at, and where I wanted to be in life. As a result, I began to frequent a Greek Orthodox monastery in Florence, Arizona. The monks there are very dedicated men to prayer and hard labor. They live a simple life. They farm to sustain themselves. I have found those monks to be very holy and wise men. As I have drawn near to God through orthodoxy, I have more peace in my life.

This peace is giving me some clarity and direction in life. Stability is a big thing for orthodoxy and I am finding that through orthodoxy itself, and in my daily living. I am currently working and going to school. Now I live with one of my roommates who is my best friend from seminary, Pedro. He is one of the little Guatemalan-American twins that I clicked really well with at seminary. He decided he needed a change in his life and then he moved to Phoenix. Along with all of these things, I have been able to grow and my mother and I keep in regular contact. Things aren't perfect but we continue to strive to understand each other. Life is ongoing and the world doesn't stop turning for any of us, so we must keep at it.

My mother is currently living with a woman. She is set to retire in two years and she is planning on becoming a massage therapist after that. She is a naturalist, she eats healthy and tries her best to lead a balanced lifestyle. She cooks almost daily now and she has gotten much better at it. She also makes organic homemade facial-cleansing creams. She wants to start a business where she can sell natural remedies and facial masks. Mom is extremely knowledgeable about skin and health. Mom has always kept up her drumming, and she even learns new songs to keep up her edge. I love to see her having healthy outlets and hobbies that she can resort to decompress a little. She dreams of visiting Hawaii one day, I would love to see her check that off on her bucket list. She is becoming a more fulfilled person, and I would love to see her accomplish her goals in life. My mother has matured tremendously in the last three years. Sometimes we still lash out to one another in conversation, but we return to the stillness and calmness pretty quickly.

My mother is unique so I am constantly learning about her and understanding her. We have conversations that range from common and ordinary things to the deep spiritual things. Our interactions are meaningful now. She is becoming a better mother to me. As the saying goes, "it ain't over 'til it's over." I had it rough growing up, but I cannot imagine what my mother has gone through in her life. I try to understand her, but the truth is that I can't fully do that. She has suffered many damaging things, experiences that I will never know how to endure in my own life. I cannot walk a mile in her shoes, and I can't place myself in her shoes. We can't go as far to understand what is in another person's heart completely, but we can hear their story to get a better understanding of where people are at.

Her life has been singular, so is mine, and so is everyone else's. In a way, if we are all singular, then no one is special. The world keeps turning, and we can't stop it. So we have to get busy with living. However, I can be a supportive son as she is a supportive mother. She is growing closer to Christ, and one helpful thing she does for herself is read Joyce Meyer books. Since our rough patches we have grown leaps and bounds, she says the following about our relationship as mother and son,

"Since everything that has happened, my emotional wounds have begun to heal. My life has become joyous and peaceful and I'm content with myself. My son and I are closer than ever. I don't try to go back in time anymore and relive the gloomy and depressed days. I am grateful for the present day and for everyone and everything that I still have in my life. I am only looking forward now. I look to the bright future enthusiastically. I'm so thankful for having my son again, for the opportunity to love him in my life. He is so many things to me that there wouldn't enough paper to put it all down. He will make you laugh uncontrollably until your cheeks hurt, I know that he has for me. He will defend you. He is honest with himself and with others, and this will cause him to see you as a person, in the most loving way possible."

We have come to understand each other more deeply, but there is always room for growth. The more we live fully, the more we can keep discovering more about another person. I am still trying to find myself, but I am on a better footing than before. In general I have a better understanding of my life and where I'm headed. I am always discovering, I am always sifting. I want to be passionate about my life. Here's one example, I had aspired to become a commercial pilot, but fulfilling our dreams and goals take time and dedication. Upon reflecting on my past I think that many of us, millennials, have far too many options and distractions in life to find what it is that we want to do with ourselves. Life was meant to be simple, but I think it can easily become complicated. Some questions and emotions in life are complicated, so it seems that we have to get to the truth of the matter. We have to get to the core of things, and this is key for understanding yourself. In understanding yourself you will come to understand other people as well.

Since life is simple, we should cherish all of the little moments. If we do not cherish these little moments, they become missed opportunities that we are never able to recover, but we must cherish them in the moment and not as a fading memory. I have done my best to not have too many of these fleeting moments, I try to not have any regrets whatsoever. This thought brings me to reflect on the most important people in my life. Most are still with me but I have suffered some significant losses. Unfortunately during the completion of this book, on Friday February 2nd, 2018 at 3:03 p.m., my grandfather passed away due to stomach cancer. Before he died, I was able to see him. Before he received the last rites, I sat next to him and we spoke. He told me that whatever I would do in life, that he would be proud of me and that he loved me. At the very end he was unable to speak, so his last words to me were especially meaningful. I definitely wish that I could talk to him more, and to just be with him. This is a something I would like to say to him,

"You were the only father I ever had. I will never forget what you taught me in life. I will never forget mowing the church lawn together or helping you with the snow-blower. I will never forget you letting me drive your truck while I sat in your lap. I won't forget the little things that left such great memories for me. You lived a meaningful life and now your soul is with God. Love you Grandpa."

I cherished many little moments with my grandpa. These will never be lost. His death made me realize how short life can be. He was there one day and now he is gone. I can still remember his piercing green eyes. I remembered him from my childhood, and that seemed like only an instant ago. Though I have travelled extensively, the most exciting moments that I had abroad are nothing compared to the most boring moments I had with my grandpa. I think that if you have some sort of good male figure in your life, you either want to be just like them or you will fall short of achieving that. Nothing that is good will last forever in this world. We always lose the people that are closest to us. Grandpa and I butt heads and we sometimes couldn't swallow our own pride to be peaceful, but it was just our nature. In the end that didn't matter anymore. We had just lost our family patriarch. The family dynamic will never be the same. His passing was my first real experience with death. I thought that as a Christian it wouldn't faze me as much as it did, it jolted me. I tried to prepare for it logically and mentally. I didn't want to see him suffer in this life and maybe his death would bring relief to him. I am glad he is not suffering, but he is missed. When someone so close passes away, a hug from the ones remaining becomes that much more significant. In that bitterness the rest of life can become sweeter.

I am learning more about my strengths and weaknesses. My grandfather's death has made me realize the brevity of life and how important it is to live as best as we can. It is like closing your eyes and savoring a good meal. We have to enjoy those simple things. Eventually the meal is up, and we are gone from this world. Mom and I now have that in mind and we can move on forward from here.

I have many worries as I have mentioned before, my mom has her own view on sexuality and this could be incompatible with my life in general. After the priesthood didn't become the definitive option for me, I now have the dilemma of how having a lesbian mom will pan out with my future family. I am on the search for my true love in life. I worry about how the dynamic would go with my future wife's family. I wonder if they would accept me, and if they would accept my mother. Yes, she would be marrying me, but it seems that comes along with the history and background and everything else that I am. Sometimes I feel at my wit's end about this question. There are many worries but I try to keep life simple. We all suffer loss and pain, but we can only move forward from there.

IN THE END: JOURNEY CONTINUES...

In moving forward we must never forget to be thankful for what cards we've been dealt. We were all dealt a hand, so we have to play. We might as well be thankful and enjoy it a little. There would definitely be something missing in my life if I couldn't mature enough to be grateful for what I have today. It is not being conformist to be happy with what we have in our lives, it's vital to enjoy what we have. In discovering more of who my mom is, I have been able to discover myself more deeply, and to have an honest look at everyone I encounter.

Relationships can be sweet, but they are not an easy thing to maintain because they require daily effort. We invest a lot into our relationships, or at least we are expected to invest in them, in order for them to be good and healthy. Relationships are a lot of give and take. Most of the give and take begins with dialogue, the starting point. We are capable of doing things to each other that are unspeakable, but once they can have some light shed on them, then these unspoken pains or these secrets have no power. The shrouded becomes uncovered, the unspoken becomes spoken. We would be kidding ourselves if we thought that our marriages, our fatherhood, our motherhood our brotherhood, or our sisterhood would be in good condition without investing ourselves. What has helped for me was to put a little distance between myself and my family so I could be more independent. I wasn't in control of anyone else, and I will never be. I was supposed to assume my role as a son and grandson, that was the key to bridging the gaps between our lives. The key is to fully be who we are, to become who we really are. I now understand that we are born into our families and that is not something we get to choose, but we can always reshuffle the cards that we are dealt, and play our hand.

We shouldn't give up hope, and I know I have given hope up before, but hope is never dead. The only hope we should give up is the hope for a better past… So let's flip it. If our past was difficult, it at least served to make us stronger. It also serves as valuable experience. We just have to find the truth in everything in our lives. I must say that I agree with Friedrich Nietzsche on this one, "That which doesn't kill us, makes us stronger." I don't agree with many of his ideas, but I give credit where it is due. Don't fold, keep playing the game. We are dealt cards and that is beyond our control there is no denying that, but why not seek reconciliation with one another, if it's a possibility? Forgiveness is from one person to another and it is important to distinguish this between reconciliation. I only came to understand this lesson after all of the craziness of my childhood.

Everyone one of us should learn to forgive and to ask for forgiveness. We can't be pushovers though, and there will be times in our lives that we shouldn't apologize for how we live our lives, if we are living right. Everyone has the capacity to forgive, but reconciliation is a harder work to accomplish. It is more difficult because reconciliation is a two way street. I may not reconcile with everyone that I have hurt and offended throughout the years, but I sure hope that you can forgive me if I did. This goes for any bad experience or relationship, whether romantic or between family members. I would just like for you to understand where I am coming from. I don't justify any wrong that I may have done, if you can understand me then that is great. If you cannot understand me, I realize it takes time and I can be patient. I have made it a personal view of mine to be understanding of other people. I grew up with deceit and a timidity to be who I really am, so I want that to end in my life here. My hope with this story, that you can do the same in your life. As I stated earlier, reconciliation is a two way street, but I had a lot of help before I realized this. I hope that this work of mine will be the help that you may need in your life.

My grandparents always have taught me Christian values and these same values steadily became a bigger part of my identity. At sometimes more than others. My grandparents are somewhat simple folk, but with their simplicity they taught me that virtues are not abstract concepts, rather they are supposed to be expressed concretely with our words and actions. I hold so much of them inside of me. Their influence in my life has been indispensable. My grandfather is now gone, and my grandmother remains with us here. I have lost my grandpa and I know what it is to lose a person so dear to me. Now when I am with my loved ones I speak from the heart. I would like to share the following words of gratitude with her:

Dear Grandma,
"You are the hidden angel in all this. You are the simplest and kindest person I know. You have always been by my side. Even when I feel the whole world is against me, I know in my heart that you are there. I remember when Grandpa and I would get into a fight, and after we would make up and be fine, he would say "You know Daniel... I'm sorry. I don't mean to say the things I said, forgive me, you know I'm not perfect, and neither are you but the only perfect person I know is grandma." Thanks for teaching me by your quiet example. I love you glo-mo!"

Understanding, love, forgiveness, just to use a few examples, all have a face. They all have a place where they are born. These virtues took on my mother's face and my own face as well. During my time at seminary I would call her more and I began to miss her more when I wasn't around her. It was then that I realized I needed to be a better son.

Concurrently she felt the same, and knew that she needed to be a better mother. That was pure grace. That is when we began to connect, but it took some working towards before we could make it happen. Yes I went through hell, yes I suffered loneliness, yes I grew angry and resentful, and yes my past did shape me in some ways throughout my childhood that still affect me today, but I still love my mother. Yes, we have some baggage but that doesn't sum us up as people. She is enough as is, and I am enough to her as well. When love is difficult and it requires a true choice, that is when it is most valuable, that is when it is most an unconditional love. Though my mom and I don't see eye to eye on many things, it has been crucial for us to be open and honest with one another. We respect each other. We have clearly defined that nothing else matters more than this. This allows us to truly love each other. I accept her for who she is, my mother. Once this truth set in, how could I shun her? Today we have discussions all the time, we call each other frequently, and we always share with each other how we are doing in our lives.

My experience has taught me all of this, but there are some key takeaways that are helping me develop myself further, and I would like to share them with you. If we can't change the circumstances, maybe we need to change our attitude. Without our personal trials, how can love and understanding follow us? It is only with these tests that love and understanding can truly be authentic. It doesn't mean to tolerate what we shouldn't in another person, nor does it mean to ignore another person's faults so that ours can be ignored as well. It means to get to know each other, it takes getting to the core of people. What has helped us is living deeply, and not being superficial with one another. On this note, I want to express my love for her in the following words,

Dear Mom,
"I love you. I know that is not the first thing I should say in a letter because it seems overused, however it is true. I have always loved you and I believe that this love between a mother and son can never be broken. There were times where I thought I didn't love you and I blamed you for all the shit that was in my life. It was the easy thing to do, to play the blame game. You never listened to me. I was always on the back burner because of your search for true love. I was never

enough for you. My smile, my heart, and just me, I was never enough. Because of your actions you caused me to cry and scream to God and ask of him, why? Why won't my mom love me? Why won't she defend me? At times I simply wished to be annihilated, no heaven, no hell, to just cease to exist. However, what I went through is nothing compared to the pain and suffering you endured, and sometimes it still haunts you to this day. I know you have also asked God "Why me?" I remember the day you told me you were molested, it left a lasting effect on my outlook. I literally felt my heart sink and I began to cry for you. It was at this moment that I realized I didn't really know you. I did not know your brokenness nor did I know how deeply you were hurt. I still can't fathom it. I know you feel guilty, and you carry this guilt. My only wish and prayer is that you are freed from this guilt and from being paralyzed and co-dependent. Now, every day I wish I could hug you and make you feel whole again and erase the pain. Perhaps that's impossible, but I will spend the rest of my days trying. Remember a few years ago, I told you that you have a life of a saint? I believe this still rings true. Love you mom."

We can't erase our pain from the past, but that is all where it is supposed to be, in the past. That is not to say that we won't have more trials come out, there are still more to come, and maybe even greater ones as I am maturing as a man. No one is one-hundred percent ready for life, but it is life itself that helps strengthen us. Life happens, so we have to live it. My mom's and my own inability to dialogue, among other things in life, has taken years away of love, understanding, and peace already. Some ideas are irreconcilable but we all can work on reconciliation. How could we let it take any more time away from us. The way I had experienced my mom's open sexuality and the way that she experienced my judgement on her sexuality, caused a significant rift between us. I think that outside a person's core there is always room for improvement, but I couldn't demand growth if I hadn't begun this from within my own self. I am referring to my sonship towards my mother, and to her motherhood towards me. What should be understood is that there is room to consider a person's sexuality because this shouldn't be ignored. There is room to consider religious and spiritual beliefs because, when dealing with people especially our loved ones, these things shouldn't be ignored. All of these things do add to a person, but all of these things do not yet get to the core of a person, not even our shortcomings. I am not suggesting that we should just keep up appearances and follow a ruse. No! We are dealing with people. So we must act accordingly.

Once I could look beyond all of the externals, once I could see beyond all of the things that are on the surface of my mother's core, then we are just looking at another 'self.' When looking someone in their eyes you will find exactly that, another 'you.' Our differences are still differences, but my mom and I couldn't let these keep us estranged from each other even further. We can harm each other in unspeakable ways but we can also begin to love each other similarly, in a way that words really can't express. We can grow in love, and this I have done. My mom has intentionally done this with me as well.

We are also still healing. It was not a onetime occurrence where we were completely healed of our wounds and mistakes. It takes time to heal, but not only time, it takes vulnerability. As a child, I didn't want to be honest and vulnerable. So what changed? A person that I admire much, Tony Robbins, said something that resonates deeply with me. "Heal the boy, and the man will appear." My mother and I have both experienced this for ourselves. We can all be deeply wounded, outright rejected, on the other hand we can heal in a way that corresponds directly with these same wounds. It was many things really, but it was periodic reflection on my journey that made me realize something was off. Once I realized this, all it took for us was to put ourselves out there. Yeah, my mom is a lesbian, but she is my mother. I love her and she loves me, and I thank God I grew up with her.

ABOUT THE AUTHOR

Hello everyone, I'm D. E. Cupertino and I am a millennial, without a man-bun, that is. I am simply a grass-roots kind of guy. I was raised in rural Arizona by my grandparents and my mother, they being deeply Catholic people and my mother being a lesbian, it was an interesting dynamic, to say the least. Though I am an independent person, both of these influences played significant roles in molding me as I am today. I grew up a single child and this helped me to become even more autonomous. I have been working on my book project for the last year in the hopes that it will have a decent impact on the world to serve humanity.

WWW.DECUPERTINO.COM

www.ingramcontent.com/pod-product-compliance
Lightning Source LLC
Chambersburg PA
CBHW072017040426
42447CB00009B/1656